AF231396

A Life You Want

Take Charge of Your Life!

Vanessa E. Kelman

WORD COLLAGE PUBLISHING

Contents

Novels by
Vanessa E. Kelman

Introduction

Life doesn't always go as we had hoped or planned. Situations out of our control affect not only our day-to-day lives but also our overall outlook and the opportunities we have. Our personalities change and shift, changing our perspectives and priorities. Relationships ebb and flow, leading to potentially drastic changes in our lives.

Sometimes these changes are for the best. They can lead to growth and new opportunities. But sometimes change can be painful, damaging to our bodies, minds, and spirits. If you're reading this book, I'm willing to bet that you're experiencing some of that discomfort, even if you're not quite sure how it happened or how to return to contentment. Hopefully this book can help. Hopefully my experiences and research can guide you on a journey of self-reflection and productivity as you figure out what needs to change and how to change it.

This book stems from the blog A Life You Want (www.ALifeYouWant .com). It is drawn from the posts that compiled the first year of the blog. Visit the site now, and you will find not only the blog, but also tools and resources to help you in your journey. You can also find motivation and connection on our Facebook page, at www.Facebook.com/ALifeYouWant.

Both the blog and the book are broken down into seven parts: Getting Started, Money, Career, Health, Relationships, Making a Difference, and Staying Motivated, and this book tackles each of them in turn, with each further divided into chapters focusing on more specialized topics. Read straight through or skip around to the sections that speak to you. Keep in mind that this book is meant to be a starting point, to give you a push to take charge of your own life, to create a life you want. You will find additional resources recommended throughout, but I encourage you to explore your own world to see what you find, too. Don't let the limits of this book limit your dreams. Just about anything is possible!

It's going to be an exciting journey. It's been exciting and invigorating for me, and I know it can be for you, too. So give it some time, think about what you want, and let's get started!

Disclaimer

The tips, ideas, and suggestions that are made in this book (and the coordinating website) are based on my personal experiences and knowledge. While they are based on sound information, I am not an expert or medical professional. For specific medical, psychological, or legal concerns, I encourage you to seek out a professional in the appropriate field.

My Story

I took turning 30 hard. Here I was: a college graduate, married, with a house, and yet I felt as if I hadn't accomplished anything in my life. I had a failed business; I had tried out several different careers with no success; my completed novel "wasn't what they were looking for;" and I was struggling with starting a family. I felt like a big, fat failure.

When that big day approached, I was a little emotional. I did my best to hide it from friends and family, but inside I was a mess. Once the day passed, however, and I was able to look at things a bit more objectively, I realized: hey, I'm still young. So what if I haven't accomplished what I wanted to? Just because it hadn't happened yet doesn't mean it wouldn't happen.

So I made it happen. I took charge of my life.

That was in 2010. Since then, a lot has changed! After more trial and error, I've found a career that brings me fulfillment. I've also self-published five novels, with more in the works. I've started new projects that bring me joy and excitement. While my marriage didn't work out, we're amicable, and before divorcing we had two beautiful children who test my patience but bring me pride and satisfaction. I've made strides in getting my finances in order, making a difference in the lives of others, and figuring out how to reach health goals.

The path has not always been easy. At times it's been a definite struggle. But that's life. I know it will always consist of ups and downs. The important part – the part that drew me to creating the blog and this book – is knowing that I'm happier, closer to where I want to be, than ever before. I'm still working on reaching total contentment, and I'm still dealing with unexpected challenges, but I know I can get there. A positive mindset and willingness to put in the work have served me well.

Are you ready to join me?

Part One

Getting Started

Chapter 1

Taking Charge

Taking charge of your life is hard. Not only do you have to figure out what you want; you have to figure out how you're going to get it. You have to set goals, make game plans, and stay motivated to keep going. But, while it may be difficult, it's worth it. The goal is your dream, the life you want.

When it comes to visualizing a journey, a mountain peak is often a representation of reaching your goal, and it can be an accurate comparison. It's a hard climb up, but once you've reached the summit, what a view! On the way up, however, you'll encounter obstacles galore. Some will be outside forces taking their toll on you, physically and mentally. Some will be internal struggles, battling you from the inside, holding you back. The road is long, difficult, challenging.

The worst, however, is the lack of oxygen as you proceed. The higher you get — the closer you get to your goals — the harder it is to breathe. Challenges get even harder. Your body is put under stress. You get lightheaded, unsure if you can make it. It takes more effort just to take another step. What do you do?

Some will succumb to the pressure and begin the descent back down. Perhaps they don't want to reach their goal strongly enough to put forth the effort required.

Some will think themselves weak, and while they really want to reach the peak, they don't think they're strong enough to make it. They hem and haw at their current level, unsure what to do, perhaps eventually making their way down over time.

The rest, though — the achievers — will take as deep a breath as they can and keep going. They acknowledge it won't be easy to get to the top, but reaching it is the only option. Perhaps they have something to prove — to themselves, to others. They want to know they were able to succeed. They want to have the satisfaction, the pride, that reaching their goal will provide. Or perhaps they simply understand that the alternative is just not acceptable. A discouraging, mediocre life is not the way to happiness.

Which category do you fall into? Are you determined enough to be one of the elite, reaching your goals and living the life you want? Or do you lack the determination and strength to make it to the top? We're all capable of reaching that peak. But you need to believe in yourself for it to happen. It won't be easy. But if you believe in yourself, you *will* reach your goals.

Chapter 2

SETTING GOALS AND MAKING PLANS

No matter what you're trying to achieve, setting goals will help keep you focused and on track to achieve it. But not knowing how to reach your goals will ensure you stay stuck in your rut, spinning your tires, frustrated with no progress. That's where making plans comes into play. This chapter will cover both.

Making goals and plans that are in alignment with what you really want and who you are will set you up for success, making it easier to stay motivated and get where you want to be.

Setting Goals

You likely have a picture in your mind of your ideal life, filled with everything you've ever wanted. That image is where you want to be, but it's probably not very specific. You need to determine what that life is like, and which aspects of it are different from the life you have now, so you can figure out how to get to that point.

What is it you're ultimately hoping to achieve by taking charge of your life? If you need help deciding, check out the other parts of this book or visit the blog at www.ALifeYouWant.com to get ideas and inspiration.

The purpose is to figure out which aspects of your life you want to change, and how you want them to change. What is your desired end result? That is your dream.

Once you have your dream in place, you need to determine how to get there. What do you want to accomplish and when? That is your goal, and depending on what you want to change, you may have multiple.

Write down your goals, as this will provide visual motivation whenever you question what you're doing or why. While you're formulating these goals, however, make sure you take a few things into consideration:

Make Them Smart

Have you ever heard of S.M.A.R.T. goals? Each letter stands for a quality your goals should have, with the intent of making your goal as achievable as possible. S.M.A.R.T. breaks down into:

S – Specific – Make sure your goal indicates exactly what you want rather than a vague idea. For example, "get healthy" doesn't indicate the qualities necessary to be considered healthy. Unless your goal is specific, you won't know what you're striving for. Do you need to improve your diet? Exercise? Get your blood pressure under control?

M – Measurable – Your goal should have a target you're trying to reach, such as how much you want to have in your emergency fund or how much weight you want to lose. Saying "save money" or "lose weight" doesn't let you know what your actual goal is. Without an actual target, you won't know when or if you've reached your goal.

A – Achievable or Attainable – In other words, realistic. I'll go more into that in the next section. You need to actually be *able* to reach your goal in order to reach your goal. If you set something too lofty, you're setting yourself up for disappointment. That doesn't mean you shouldn't dream big. It just means you may need to adjust timelines or create smaller goals on the way to reaching your ultimate goal.

R – Relevant – Make sure your goal aligns with what you're actually hoping to accomplish. If you're hoping to get healthier, but the goals you're setting focus more on how much you spend on meals rather than what those meals consist of, you may need to adjust your focus.

T – Time-Bound or Timely – Having a goal is great, but without any kind of deadline you may find it hard to stay motivated. What's the rush? Indicating *when* you want to reach your goal can give you that push to stay on track.

By keeping your goals S.M.A.R.T., you'll get that much closer to the life you want. Now let's take things a little further.

Be Realistic

As with any goals, to set yourself up for success you should set realistic expectations. Lose 10 pounds in a month? Doable. Lose 50 pounds a month? Not so much. Get a job? Doable. Get a highly competitive job you'll love in less than a month in a bad economy? That's a bit harder. Take a look at your ultimate goals, your habits, and your lifestyle. What can be done when all factors are taken into consideration? What can be done with reasonable modifications?

Take Life Into Consideration

Things happen. Life happens. Not taking that into account when setting your goals can be a death sentence. For example, setting a strict regimen for yourself that requires things happening at the same time every day can be difficult — especially if your work schedule changes, you have a spouse and/or children, or you have any kind of commute that can be affected by traffic.

Take Others Into Consideration

Unless you live by yourself in a bubble, you'll have to interact with other human beings. Whether those people are friends, family members, coworkers, or even casual acquaintances, they have the ability to affect your life. Relationships take time, and interactions take time, and, regardless of the level of closeness, each person you interact with will take time. That affects the time you have to devote to your goals and resolutions.

In addition, some of the things you decide to do or change can have an effect on these other people. For example, if you decide you want to move to a warmer climate to a state with a lower cost of living, you'd better hope your spouse and kids are on board — or they'll fight you every step of the way.

Go For Wants Instead of Shoulds

I should eat healthier. But unless I get to the point where I *want* to, staying motivated will remain a challenge — and will probably mean I won't be successful. If you focus on what you *should* be doing, or *should* be resolving to do, maintaining any kind of life change will be difficult. You'll dread doing what you need to do to reach your goal. And that means you'll "cheat." You'll slack off. You'll come up with reasons not to. In short, you won't reach your goal. Instead, focus on the life changes you *want* to make. If you're tired of eating junk food and want to eat healthy, to feel healthy, then you'll be more motivated to succeed. And that means it'll be easier to reach your goals. Besides, shouldn't the life you want consist of what you actually want?

Create a Life You Want

Most importantly, make sure you're making changes for the right reasons. If you reach your goal, will you be happy? Or are you doing something just to make someone else happy? This is *your* life, and you're the one who has to live it. Be sure that any changes you make will bring you that much closer to creating a life *you* truly want.

Making Plans

Once you know where you want to be, you have to figure out how you're going to get there. Having a game plan in place to determine your steps can keep you on track and make sure you don't get lost, or procrastinate from not knowing what to do.

Below I describe my process, and recommendations for creating a series of lists and plans to help you achieve your goals. You are, of course, welcome to develop a system that works for you. I actually encourage it. Take what you can from my process, think about how you work, how you stay organized, and what motivates you, and establish a plan that really speaks to you. Trying to adhere to a course of action that doesn't work for you will only result in frustration and failed attempts. Consider this a starting point.

My first step is taking my desired end result and figuring out what I would need to do to get there. Let's take a simple example: to become debt free, I need to pay off each credit card bill and avoid charging additional items. Simple enough. I list each credit card I need to pay off. Then I break it down even further: how much do I owe on each card? what's the interest rate on each one? When it comes to the second part, avoiding additional charging, I try to figure out where I can cut back on spending so we're not living beyond our means. Are there bills I can lower? Expenses I can cut?

Each one of the items on this new list becomes a mini goal, and I can break it down even further. How am I going to pay off those bills? Will I establish a debt snowball to pay them off in time? Will I look at changing energy suppliers to cut my electric bill? Cut out unneeded items on our cell phone bill? If I normally go out for coffee every day or purchase new clothes regularly, can I cut back on that unnecessary spending?

The things I come up with become my to-do list. Some items I may need to break down further as I go along, but for now I at least have an actionable list. And once I've got a concrete idea of what I'm going to do, I put it into effect. I take the things I've decided to do and do them.

I look into changing energy suppliers and select one. I reduce our cell phone data plans. I determine how much I'll pay each month toward my credit card bills. Each action will take me closer to my goal, and I can check things off my to-do list. If there are items I'm trying *not* to do, I can put those on my to-do list for each day or week or month, too: i.e. pass Starbucks without stopping.

When I do the items on my to-do list will vary. Some things, such as actually paying off the credit card bills, will get done according to my bill-paying schedule (more on that in Part Two). Other things I fit in as I have the time. Sometimes I'll take my work schedule for the week or month and actually write in when I'll do things, according to when I have a morning or day off.

Since I have many goals going at once, my schedule gets quite full. To keep myself somewhat organized, I will sometimes plan out every spare moment. Sometimes this will consist of a general goal for the day or time slot (for example "update website"). Other times I will give myself specific tasks (i.e. make a particular phone call, run an errand, etc.). (Tip: If you choose to plan out your entire day or week, be sure to schedule in downtime and self-care!)

Having it all written down helps keep me accountable and focused. It's harder to slack off without guilt if I know I had things scheduled. And, ultimately, the purpose is to move forward in my goals. The only way to do that is to move forward with my course of action. And, for me, that's checking things off my to-do list.

Managing Your Time

When it seems as though every spare moment is already filled with something that just has to get done, you may ask yourself how you will possibly add more to the to-do list. The answer, I find, lies not in finding more time but in managing the time you have. If you pay attention to what you spend your time doing, chances are you can find a better way to get things done. Perhaps it's a question of lumping similar items together (such as running errands or doing paperwork). Perhaps it's a question of getting rid of those time wasters you don't even realize you spend so much time with (social media? emails? games on your phone?).

Try tracking how long it takes you to get certain tasks done. Pay attention to how much time you spend watching TV, checking Facebook, etc. While some downtime is important, are you really getting any enjoyment from mindless doom scrolling? Could you be putting that time to better use? Once you've seen what you spend time doing, think of what you *want* to spend your time doing. Are there certain to-do items or steps toward your goal that you never seem to have time for?

Next, it's time to prioritize. What has to get done right away? What has to get done at some point each day? What has to get done eventually? And what can be done away with completely? Create a routine for yourself that fits in with these priorities. I have found that routines not only make me feel more in control, but they also free up more time and mental energy. I know when I'm going to get things done, so I don't have to worry about it. It's not one more thing to think about. And knowing when I'm getting things done means I don't waste time figuring out what I'm doing next, or what has to get done, or what's more important.

While establishing your routine, think about what can be done simultaneously. Multi-tasking can be a great resource if done properly. For example, toss in a load of laundry before you start your paperwork, and you're magically getting two things done at once! Or if there's a TV show you absolutely must watch, try filing or doing research online while you're watching it.

You can also save time by making lists of things to buy or places to go and getting all your errands done at once without having to worry about forgetting something. Try planning ahead for your meals so prep time is shortened. Stock up on items when you find them on sale so you're not running out at the last minute on wasted trips to the store.

Determine your goals, come up with a game plan, and find the most efficient way of getting things done, and you'll be well on your way to success.

Moving Past Planning

So you've got lists, ideas, and courses of action. You know where you're going and how you're going to get there. But it all doesn't mean a thing if you don't *do* something. In the next chapter we'll discuss putting the plan into action.

Chapter 3

STEPS TO SUCCESS

Coming up with a game plan can sometimes be the easy part. Executing said game plan is often the challenge. How do you get from point A to point B?

Step 1: Use What You've Got

If you've got it, flaunt it, right? Well, when it comes to making changes in your life, if you've got it, utilize it. This could be time, money, people, resources — anything that can help you in your new mission. Here are some examples:

- You want to find a new career, so you tell everyone you know (utilizing your friends and acquaintances)

- You want to earn more money to get out of debt, so you spend your weekends mowing lawns and raking leaves (utilizing your spare time)

- You want to repair your relationship with your mother, so you enlist your younger brother — who has a close relationship with Mom — to help (utilizing your family members)

- You want to lose weight, so you scour your cabinets and cookbooks to find low-fat recipes and ideas (utilizing your resources)

- You want to make a difference in children's lives, so you spend a couple of nights a week coaching a basketball team. You also take some of your personal funds to purchase uniforms and equipment for the team (utilizing your spare time and money)

With these ideas as a starting point, what do you have that you can utilize to get you moving in the right direction?

Time

Time can be your greatest resource, and using the time you've got can be a valuable way to get what you want. As we discussed in the previous chapter, managing your time can ensure you're able to move ahead in your goals. In the examples above, time was used to take action on changes you want to make. Time can also be used to research, network, or plan out a course of action. Putting time to good use will move you forward more than anything else.

If time is already tight, see where you can cut back on activities that are less important to you. Or search for pockets of time, such as a lunch break, to get things done, such as looking for a new job, searching for healthy recipes, or researching volunteer opportunities.

Money

If what you want to change is in the money category, this may not be a plentiful resource to use. But before you dismiss it completely, take a look at your finances and make sure you're really putting your money to its best use. Are you wasting money on eating out? Frivolous purchases? Special features on your cell phone or cable bill that you don't use? Redirect your money so it better aligns with your goals.

If money is not an issue for you, then perhaps it can help you in your mission: fund education to advance your career, enlist the help of a counselor to help with your family or relationship troubles, hire a personal trainer to help in weight loss or working out goals, donate to a charity that means a lot to you. The only limit is your imagination (and your bank account!).

People

Your friends, family, and acquaintances can also be a valuable tool when it comes to advancing your goals. Telling everyone you know can give you a kick in the tush when it comes to keeping you on track. But talking to them about your changes can also provide you with support, information, and leads on new ideas and opportunities, as well. This is called networking, and many people will tell you it's the only way to get ahead. Even if you don't know how to get a foot in the door at a particular place of employment, or you're not familiar with the latest medical breakthrough, a friend of a friend might. And that's a very powerful tool to have in your belt. In addition, simply talking to others about your changes can encourage ideas that you wouldn't have had otherwise.

When you're accepting the help of other people, however, make sure you're not taking advantage of them. Just as they can help you, you may be able to help them. Keep your eyes and ears open for any opportunities that can help someone you know, and be willing to lend an ear to someone else who needs to discuss making changes, too. Networking is a two-way street.

Resources

Just about anything else can fall into this category. In the example I used above, I mentioned using tangible items — food and cookbooks that you already had — to guide you. But even intangible items can help you in your mission. For example, you may have the internet at your fingertips, and the internet offers a wealth of information on any subject imaginable. Using it to research what you want to change can give you tons of ideas. Likewise, the library and the people who work there can provide information and leads on a variety of subjects.

More abstractly, consider taking a walk to clear your head. This can free your mind to problem solve and think more creatively. Listen to music. Paint a picture. Doodle. Your greatest resources is your brain — use it!

Step 2: Think Positively

Once you're taking advantage of everything you currently have as resources, you'll want to take it one step further and look for opportunities that present themselves.

As a general rule, people tend to fall into two categories: pessimists and optimists. Those who see the glass half empty (pessimists) will likely look for reasons they aren't successful. There's always an excuse for failure: the economy is terrible, I'm under a lot of stress, my boss is out to get me, all the good ones are taken. While some good things may happen to these people, they may be too busy complaining to even notice. Or they may taint the experience with phrases like "it's about time."

Those who see the glass half full, however, (optimists) will see the silver lining on every experience. And that means they'll find the opportunities that lie in each situation. Even less-than-ideal experiences are opportunities for improvement. And the true opportunities — those that present themselves regularly, if one pays attention — can be taken advantage of.

Try to look at your life a bit more objectively. Examine experiences from different angles to see if perhaps there's a way you can benefit. Is there a different way of doing things? Are you missing something that could benefit you? Is there someone you can network with who can help you? Is there an experience you can gain that can help you in the long run? Simply trying out different perspectives can reap huge rewards.

The more you push yourself to look at positive alternatives, the more natural it will become. Instead of automatically thinking the worst, you'll start looking at all options, and then, perhaps, the more positive. And with that new outlook comes a greater ability to succeed. Then, when big opportunities present themselves, you'll be primed to take advantage. You'll be able to acknowledge and appreciate the gift you're being given — and you'll be able to use it to your benefit. It's a self-fulfilling prophecy. If you believe you'll be successful, you will be. If you don't, then you won't be.

While you're at it, don't forget to be grateful for what you have. When an opportunity *does* present itself, be grateful. When things go your way, express thanks. Let the people in your life know you appreciate them.

When we're optimistic and grateful, we're more giving, more loving, more appreciative, more upbeat. Gratitude makes us *live*. We look at the world differently. Rather than just stuff, we're surrounded by belongings, tokens of all that we really have. We share experiences with those we love, and we're grateful for the time shared. We savor the moments.

All of this puts us in the right frame of mind to be happy, confident, and motivated. And then we can be successful not only on the surface, but within.

Step 3: Build Knowledge

Hopefully you're able to see and appreciate what you have, and you're able to acknowledge opportunities and experiences that come your way. But to get ahead, you'll also need to learn, to gain the skills, experiences, and information you'll need to thrive in your goals.

Knowledge is power. The more you know, the more skills you've gained, the more information you've absorbed, the greater the chances are that you'll be able to reach your goals. Knowledge isn't just about facts and figures; it's about how things work, how they go together, how they affect each other. It's about skills and problem solving and experiences.

You constantly have opportunities to learn. Whether it's at work, in life, at home, or just about anywhere, you're being exposed to new experiences, new people, new ways of doing things, that can change the way you look at something or the way you think about something. Even the smallest change can start a domino effect that results in huge breakthroughs in your thought process. And the more you know, the more you absorb, the more chain reactions you'll set off. Talk about power! Imagine being able to look at something differently and suddenly being able to solve that problem you thought was impossible. Imagine trying to do something over and over only to make a small tweak and find yourself successful.

Beyond normal experiences, however, you can also take charge and learn even more. Read books and magazines. Watch videos. Partner with others. Practice. Write it out. Think it out. Brainstorm. Jumpstart your brain to better absorb the stimuli that attack you on a daily basis.

Most important of all: leave yourself open to learn. Welcome the things that happen to you, good or bad. Process them. Learn from them. Take what you can away from them. Build your knowledge base to build your power — and build your chances of success.

A Step Further

If you need help, look for a mentor. No matter what you're aiming to change, chances are someone has traveled a similar path. And having that someone guide you, teach you, and show you what to do can help you even more.

Mentors come in all shapes and sizes, and depending on how many goals you're working on, you may have several. Often a mentor will be someone who succeeded in the area you're working on, such as a particular career path or health goal. That person will be able to suggest courses of action, let you know what worked or didn't work for him or her, and answer any questions you may have. Mentors can also be great sounding boards when it comes to ideas you have to reach your goals. Just make sure that your mentor is someone who can be both sympathetic and firm. You don't need a babysitter; you need someone who will give you a little push when you need it.

So where do you find a mentor? Well, it depends on your goal, but also how far you want to take the relationship. Many people make a living off of helping others reach their goals, whether they're financial goals, relationship goals, or just about anything else. If that's the kind of relationship you're looking for, then search online or ask friends and family for recommendations as to who to turn to. These consultants and advisors can get pricey, so do your homework and make sure that's what you really want before jumping in.

If you're looking for a more personal, laid-back relationship with a mentor, start with your friends and family. Have any of them succeeded with a similar goal? Can they recommend someone who has? If not, broaden your search. Join clubs and organizations related to your goal and look for others who have succeeded within. You can also search blogs and forums online to touch base with potential mentors.

How do you ask someone to be your mentor? Start by asking questions. If the person seems willing and able to help — and you like how they present the answers — ask if they would be willing to help in a broader, more long-term way. Many people would be honored to be asked to be a mentor. Perhaps someone helped them, and they want to pay it forward. Or perhaps they just want to help others succeed. No matter the reason, acknowledge and appreciate the help.

If someone is not willing to take on the responsibility, that's okay. Try someone else. Plenty of people are able to help. Just keep your eyes and ears open for someone who may be your perfect match.

Step 4: Take Chances

It seems like every successful person credits his or her success to taking a chance. If they had played it safe, then they wouldn't have gotten nearly as far in life. If you think about it, it's probably true: if they had just been satisfied with the status quo; if they had just punched in and punched out at their job; if they had just shrugged their shoulders and said there was nothing they could do about it; then they probably wouldn't have made incredible strides in their lives. They had to take a chance, put themselves out there, and really push themselves to become successful.

To make progress in your goals — and your life — you'll have to take some chances. They say the definition of insanity is doing the same thing over and over again and expecting different results. The same is true of success. If you simply do the same things, complete the same tasks, go to the same places, the same results will happen. To expect otherwise isn't logical. To get different results, you need to do something different. You need to break the cycle. You need to take a chance.

Taking that first step can be intimidating. Routine is very comforting. They call it your "comfort zone" for a reason! But to be successful, to lead an extraordinary life, you need to break out of that comfort zone. It can be a small step at first. Just try breaking a routine. Instead of going to a particular coffee shop for your morning coffee, for example, try someplace new. Try a new recipe for dinner. Watch a different kind of movie. Read a different kind of book. Once you've gotten used to making small changes, try something bigger...then bigger...then even bigger.

While it can be intimidating, it can also be exhilarating. It doesn't take something extreme to change your life. Even a minor shift can reap extraordinary rewards.

Of course, not all changes will bring positive results. But even less-than-ideal results can move you forward. You can learn from your mistakes, get a different perspective, get to know your limits. Even successful people make mistakes!

Leaps of Faith

Depending on your goal, and the changes you're looking to make, you may find yourself at a crossroads at some point. Do you play it safe, or do you take a chance, take a leap of faith, and hope that things will work out? When is the right time to jump?

The answer will be different for everyone, and when you find yourself at such a crossroads, the way you feel then will likely be different than what you feel now. Perspective is everything. Weigh your options, ask yourself what's the worst that could happen, and decide if you could handle it. While it can be scary, at some point a leap will need to be made. Something will need to change to move forward. How much risk are you willing to take on? What kind of reassurance would you need to take that leap of faith? When will you choose to make the jump?

Setbacks

Perhaps you find yourself checking off the easy stuff on your to do list, the quick stuff, the stuff that doesn't require too much effort. Perhaps you find yourself reluctant to do anything, either afraid or worried about what will happen when you do. Or perhaps you just keep working on your to do list, fine-tuning it until it shines, but not actually doing anything.

If you find yourself unable to take action and tackle the real meat of your plan, you may want to check out Chapter 3 in Part Seven on dealing with setbacks for tips and advice on how to move past it. Or you may just want to give yourself a push and make yourself do something of substance. Oftentimes the first step is the hardest, and getting over that hump will get you started on a productive path.

Part Two

MONEY

Chapter 1

GETTING STARTED

A h, money. Depending on who you ask, it's what makes the world go 'round or it's the root of all evil. Either way, modern life depends on it, whether we like it or not. And if you're really interested in taking charge of your money, you're probably struggling somewhat. You're not alone. Hopefully the information and suggestions in this section will help you move forward and get to a more comfortable place.

For many of us, myself included, the biggest issue is the mountain of debt. For whatever reason we find ourselves in a position where we just have too many bills and not enough income. And it can be very disheartening to be dishing out payments, especially when a good portion of those payments consists of interest. I know I've been there. I'm still there. And it will be a while before I'm completely out of it.

I won't pretend to be a financial guru. But I've read and heard lots of advice from "experts," and that, combined with what I've personally discovered and tried, has given me an idea of what will work and what won't. It's slow going, but eventually you can get yourself into a better position.

Depending on your current financial position, and what you're looking to change, you may want to focus on one or more of the following:

- Making money

- Spending money

- Saving money

- Getting rid of debt

I've created a chapter in this section for each one. Skip ahead or read straight through — it's up to you. Hopefully you'll find some tips and insight that can help you in your journey.

Before your jump in, however, evaluate your situation and try to get a handle on what's really going on and what you want to take charge of. Then, look around to determine who, besides yourself, these changes may affect.

If you're married and/or have children, the changes you plan on making will affect your family. While this holds true no matter what you're tackling, when it comes to money, the effects will be even more noticeable. It's important to make sure your spouse and children are on board with your changes. Why? A united front is a whole lot stronger than a house divided. And together your chances of success are much higher. So how do you go about doing this?

Communication

The first thing you'll want to do it *talk* to your family. Let them know about the changes you're considering, and why you think these changes are important. Let them know you want their input, and that their feedback will be taken into consideration when you're figuring out your course of action. This gets them involved and makes them feel like they're part of the team, instead of outsiders just watching the game.

Opening the lines of communication can also help encourage valuable ideas and insight you wouldn't normally have received. Looking at things from others' points of view can help you figure out which direction will be best for all of you in the long run. And getting this feedback early on will prevent backtracking later if you discover that your decisions negatively impact those around you.

Be Specific

When talking to your family, try to be as specific as possible. Rather than speaking abstractly about cutting spending or bringing down debt, discuss what exactly needs to change. Will you be eating out less? Spending less on clothing? Staying home more?

The more specific your goals, the better. Not only will it help your family understand where you're coming from and where you're going, but it will also give you a definite course of action, with a clear understanding of what you have to do to get there. And being specific in your course of action will let your family know what they have to do to be involved in the process.

Make It Fun

Making the experience interactive can bring the family together and unite you in your goals. Even if you're alone on this journey, anything that adds a little fun will help keep you motivated and on track. Try making charts or goal thermometers to track your progress. Celebrate with small rewards when you reach milestones. Reward family members if they have a great idea or do something that brings your goals closer.

You can also get the family involved in activities that directly affect the goal:

- Have everyone clear out their closets to hold a tag sale and see who will make the most

- Have a contest to see who can spend the least on school supplies or clothes

- Encourage family members to make gifts instead of buy them

— and reinforce how much more meaningful it is, in addition to saving money

Get Creative

Show everyone how being frugal can really be about being creative. Rather than depriving yourself, you're just finding different ways of doing things, and different ways of getting what you need or want:

- If you can't afford that new gadget, ask how you can use what you have to do the same thing.

- If something goes wrong in the house, learn how to fix it instead of hiring a professional. You can learn a valuable skill and save money at the same time. (Disclaimer: don't try this with big projects, especially those involving electricity, unless you already have experience or can work with someone who does. Sometimes hiring a professional will actually save you money in the long run, as well as being a much safer option.)

- For children, show them how they can use what they have and the free things around them to still have fun. Surf the internet to find craft ideas or building projects using household items.

- When something needs to be replaced, brainstorm ways to get a replacement for free or as inexpensively as possible.

Once these things become habit, you'll see how much you're actually learning and how much more valuable the entire experience has been. Instead of just dishing out money for something, you're gaining skills and experiences that will last a lifetime. Along the way you may also be keeping things out of landfills and even saving time!

Stay Positive

While it can be difficult to remain optimistic, the more hopeful and positive you can stay, the easier it will be for your family to stick with you — and the easier it will be for you to keep working on your goals. If you consider your actions a hardship, so will your family. But if you look for the fun in it, and encourage them to do the same, it will be easier for everyone to see how these changes are positive. And isn't making your lives better what it's all about?

Chapter 2

MAKING MONEY

You can't spend money if you don't have any to spend, and no matter how much you have, it seems as if it's never enough. There are regular expenses, plus the unexpected: your car broke down; your child needed braces; the water heater conked out. Or maybe you didn't believe that you needed to have money to spend it, and the debt is mounting, you want to save for a vacation, or you want to pad your savings account. Beyond the basic "get a job," what can you do to bring in more money?

If you already have a job outside the home:

- See if you can pick up a few extra hours for extra income

- Ask for a raise

- See if you're in line for a promotion

- Look for a higher-paying job in your field

You can also try to bring in supplemental income through a variety of means. If you need cash quickly, you can try selling something. Have a tag sale, post an ad on marketplace or eBay, or visit a consignment store, pawn shop, or jewelry store. You can also search for odd jobs to boost income, such as jobs found on Craigslist or Taskrabbit.

If you have a particular skill, you can use that to your advantage. Do you have experience with something, such as bookkeeping, photography, construction, or event planning? Get the word out that you're available for freelance or consulting jobs. Depending on the skill, you can try posting an ad in your local newspaper or online at sites such as Fiverr. Whatever your ability, someone is probably looking to fill a need, so think about what you can bring to the table.

If that doesn't pan out for you, or if you prefer something more consistent, you can also look for an additional job. Companies such as Uber, Lyft, and Door Dash offer the opportunity to earn extra cash in your spare time. Or you can look for a regular part-time job at retail establishments or restaurants, which tend to offer a variety of schedule options.

Another option is to pursue work-from-home opportunities. Many companies hire work-from-home staff for tasks such as data entry or other administrative duties, or for customer service. If you're interested in sales, you can also look into direct sales companies, such as Pampered Chef or PaperPie, that can lead to ongoing income, as well.

Note: No matter what you decide, keep in mind that even with on-the-side jobs, legally you must claim any income you bring in.

Other Options

In addition to jobs and selling things, you can find other ways to bring in extra funds.

Unclaimed Funds

An easy way to get extra cash is to claim what's already yours! You may have unclaimed funds, whether it's a bank account you forgot about, an insurance claim you never claimed, or any number of other sources. Whether you're struggling with money or not, don't let those unclaimed funds slip through your fingers. Start by checking out the government's unclaimed money site at https://www.usa.gov/unclaimed-money. You can also head directly to https://unclaimed.org/to conduct a search.

I personally have claimed funds found through online search sites. Several years ago, I had a health savings account. Time passed, and I stopped making deposits. Eventually the bank I had the account with closed the account due to inactivity. The money that was still in there (about $100) ended up getting sent to my state's unclaimed funds division. I eventually remembered about it and claimed the money that was rightfully mine, though the state took a cut for the trouble I put them through. If you have accounts that may have slipped into inactivity, check with your bank or your state to see if there are funds owed to you. Even if you don't think you have anything, do some quick searching. You may be surprised to find your name on the list!

Insurance Claims

Some insurance policies, such as pet insurance or accident coverage such as Aflac, require you to submit claims to get your benefits. If you don't make the claims, the company will not credit you for your expenses, and you will have paid more than you needed. Review these plans to see exactly what they cover and what documentation they require. Be sure to submit claim forms as soon as you can. Even if you have to pay a deductible or copay, getting something is better than nothing.

While you're at it, review all your insurance policies to make sure you're taking advantage of everything the policies offer. They may cover expenses you didn't know about. For example, some health insurance plans now include over-the-counter benefits. Or your plan may include categories you didn't realize, such as vision or dental, which can keep you from spending money unnecessarily. That's like finding free money!

Rebates

Whether it's a mail-in rebate from a retailer or an app that gives you cash back, rebates can add up and lead to real extra money every time you take advantage. Several apps exist that will give you cash back for purchases you already make. Some will require specific items to be purchased, while some will give a flat percentage based on the amount you spent. Check out your app store for rebate apps. Some well-known options are Rakuten, Ibotta, Fetch, and ReceiptHog. These apps will also offer bonuses and limited-time offers to get even more cash back. As a personal example, in my time using Ibotta, I've gotten over $1500 cash back.

If you prefer to shop on a desktop rather than your phone, many apps will also offer browser extensions, making it easy to activate and claim rebates. If you use Microsoft Edge as your browser, Microsoft also has their own extension, Microsoft Shopping, that can make it easy to use site coupons and get cash back.

Take Advantage

In addition to insurance policies, you may have added benefits elsewhere, too. Check with your employer's human resources department to see if there are any benefits you're not taking advantage of. Many will offer matching on retirement savings, which is not only free money upfront but will grow over time, leading to even more. One of my former employers offered an employer match and profit sharing on 401(k) accounts and 50% tuition reimbursement up to a certain amount. My current employer offers matching plus extra if I set up a retirement account. See what your employer offers and take advantage of those extra funds.

When it comes time to do your taxes, consider using specialized software or hiring an accountant to ensure you're taking advantage of all the deductions you qualify for. If you itemize your deductions, be sure to get receipts for any donations you make throughout the year so you can claim those, too.

Get creative and look around for other money-making opportunities, as well. Ask friends and family for suggestions. Just keep in mind that if something sounds too good to be true, it probably is. Always do your research and look into any opportunities that arise.

Chapter 3

SPENDING MONEY

As easily as it comes in, the money goes out. And whether you're trying to save more or looking to pay down debt, knowing where your money is going can be helpful.

Paying Bills

The biggest chunk of your paycheck is probably going toward bills. As a first step, make sure all of your bills are being paid — and paid on time. It doesn't help to add late fees to the already-high amounts or mess up your credit by having debts sent to collections.

One thing I have found to work is making a list of all my regular bills and about when they're due. I have a spiral notebook with a sheet for each month's bills. I have columns for the due date, the bill, how much is due, how much I paid, and when I paid it. For expenses that stay the same every month, I fill in the dates they're due and how much is owed. When I receive statements for the variable accounts, I fill in the appropriate columns. When I pay a bill, I fill in the amount and date paid. I can see at a glance what has and hasn't been paid, and I can see if there are any bills I didn't receive but should have. This helps me keep track, so I can see what's due when and avoid late fees.

To take the plan one step further, I've come up with a bill-paying schedule to make sure everything is getting paid on time. I have it all planned out for the whole year: when each bill is getting paid, based on how much I bring home each paycheck. To set this up, I compiled statements from the previous year and figured out when each bill is usually due, how much it's usually for, and how often they're due. Some of this was already done when I made the monthly sheets, but looking more in-depth at the statements, I was able to finagle things so I could determine when the bills would be paid, based on when they're due and when I get paid.

While it can be considerable work getting the schedule in place, it's worth it — and it does get easier each year. These efforts have made it significantly less stressful when payday comes, because I don't have to think about what I'm paying each week. I know that if I open my notebook and it says I'm scheduled to pay the electric bill and cell phone bill, that's what I'm paying. And both will be on time. Easy peasy.

While you're at it, take a good look at your bills and see what you're spending on. You may be overspending on things you don't use. Contact the billing companies and see if you can make adjustments that will save you money. (See the Saving Money chapter for more tips and info.)

The Rest of the Stuff

The little things and not-so-little things that come up on a daily or random basis can also add up. Knowing where your money is going can help you make effective changes to your habits and make progress in your saving or spending goals. By tracking your expenses, you can properly plan and decide where to cut back so you have extra money to apply toward your debt or save for your goals.

To track your expenses, carry a notepad with you and record any money you spend — whether it's 75 cents in a vending machine or a shopping spree at the mall. You may be surprised at what you spend money on and how easily it disappears. Keep the log for a week, month, or longer — however long it takes for you to see the patterns and find ways to cut back. Maybe your downfall is clothes. Can you spend less? Buy less?

Shop elsewhere? Thrift instead of buy new? Or maybe you stop at the vending machine a few times a week. Would it make more sense to buy in bulk at the store instead and bring your own snacks? Tracking your purchases can help you pick up on these quirks and guide you in ways to save.

Once you've found areas to cut back, take action. When you find yourself moving to spend that money, stop yourself and earmark that money toward your goal instead. Even 75 cents a few times a week adds up. And that can make a dent in your debt or savings goal.

If, while tracking your expenses, you find yourself spending on un-expected expenses such as car repair bills, consider starting an emer-gency fund. Put a little money aside on a regular basis so that when an unexpected bill comes up, you're ready for it. As I said above, even a small amount adds up over time. And being able to plan for saving can help make the expense more manageable than having to deal with a several-hundred-dollar bill all of a sudden.

When to Spend

With all the talk about saving money and cutting back, you may find yourself thinking that spending more than the bare minimum is never a good thing. However, that's not the case. There are many instances when spending a little — or even a lot — more makes the most sense.

Quality vs. Cost

When it comes to certain items, durability trumps cost. As such, when you're shopping for something you plan on getting a lot of use out of — a car, furniture, clothes, etc., — shop by quality level, not just price tag. While spending a lot does not necessarily mean you'll be getting the best quality, it's not often that you'll find the cheapest item to be, either. Do your research to determine which item will give you the most bang for your buck. Even if it's not cheap now, it may still save you money in the long run: you won't need to replace it as often, it will require less maintenance, and you'll spend less time dealing with hassles. Of course, if you only plan using something a few times, by all means go cheap!

Convenience

I'm all about shopping around for the best deals. And it can be very tempting to go to a million different stores because each one has the best deal on something. But keep in mind not only the cost of your time, but also the cost of gas and wear and tear on your vehicle. It doesn't make sense to go across town to save a little if you're eating up the difference in gas! Weigh the pros and cons and determine what is truly the most cost-effective option. You may end up spending a little more upfront but saving in the long run.

Memories

Perhaps the most important of all — at least in my humble opinion — is the memory factor. Material items come and go, and any money spent on them will go as well. But memories last a lifetime, and money spent on them will, too. When it comes to experiences, vacations, events, etc., consider spending a little more if it will add value to your experience. You don't have to go all out to make great memories, but you don't want your memories to be tainted by the fact that you were too cheap to do anything, either. Think about what you'll really remember and let that be your guide. The result can be the best use of your money yet.

Chapter 4

SAVING MONEY

When it comes to saving money, the chapter really needs to be split into two sections: spending less and accumulating savings. Let's start with spending less.

Spending Less

If it feels like you're spending too much, you probably are. Whether it's groceries, clothing, or household bills, there's a good chance you could make some changes that would leave a little extra cash in your pocket. Here are some tips and ideas:

Groceries

- Comparison shop — Look through sales flyers and familiarize yourself with the pricing at multiple stores. Be sure to consider not only grocery stores, but also drugstores, convenience stores, discount stores, and department stores. You may be surprised who has the best deals on certain items. For example, when I was still buying gallons of milk, I found a nearby gas station had the best price. Good to know when that's all I needed to get!

- Wait for sales — The more you do this, the better you'll get at it. Look through flyers or go online to find discounted prices on items. Don't pay full price unless you know you're getting a good deal.

- Clip coupons — Though not as prevalent as they once were, coupons are still a thing! Now, however, retailers and manufacturers utilize digital coupons more than paper. Visit websites of stores you visit, particularly stores that involve loyalty cards. Look for a "digital coupons" section on the site, peruse the offerings, and add them to your account. When you purchase a qualified item, the savings will be automatically applied. Combine coupons with sale prices to save twice as much. But resist the temptation to buy something just because you have a coupon. Figure out how much it will cost after the savings to see if it's really a good deal.

- Make a list — Knowing what you're looking for when you walk into the store will not only save you time; it will also save you money. You'll know what you need and be less tempted to grab those impulse items because you aren't walking up and down every aisle. A list will also help you stay on budget, as you can write down how much each item should cost and figure out how much you're spending ahead of time.

- Stock up — Find something you use at a great price? Will it last a while? Stock up! Not only will you save on items you use; you'll also prevent yourself from having to run out at the last minute because you ran out of something (and likely having to pay full price on it).

Clothes

- Shop thrifty — Go to thrift stores and consignment stores to pick up items at a fraction of their regular retail. Some thrift stores will also have discount days or coupons, helping you save even more. This is also a great way to get name brand or higher quality items at reduced prices.

- Outlet stores — Check out outlet stores for special deals. Familiarize yourself beforehand, however, to get an idea for how much items should cost. Even outlets can be overpriced.

- Discount stores — Discount department stores can have close-out deals on name brand items, or they can have items that may not be name brand but look almost the same at a fraction of the price. As with outlets, however, do your research. Even "discount" stores can be overpriced.

- Invest in staples — Avoid trends and purchase pieces you can wear long-term, such as classic cuts and neutral or basic colors. Then shop at the end of the season to buy clothing at a discount.

- Focus — Pay attention to the bottom line, not on how much you're "saving." And make sure you actually want and need the items you're tempted to buy. No matter how cheap, if you'll never wear it, it was wasted money.

Household Bills

- Examine — Take a good hard look at your bills. Are you paying for things you're not using? Being charged unnecessary fees? Have promotional rates expired? Talk to the companies you're working with and see what changes can be made to get rid of the excess or reduce your charges.

- Just ask — Call your credit card companies and ask to speak with a manager or someone who can give you a lower interest rate. Tell them what you bring to the table and ask them to do better on your rate. Ask utility companies about price matching from competitors. Ask cable, internet, and telephone providers about bundling or promotions. If it's a service you can get else-where or do without, let them know you're considering leaving. The worst they can say is "no."

- Shop around — Check out a variety of companies for prices on insurance, heating oil, electricity suppliers, and more. Anything with a competitor is fair game. Ask your employer if there are any companies you can get discounts through. Look around and compare.

- Downsize — Whether it's a car or a home, switching to a smaller option will likely save you money on several levels: loan pay-ments, fuel costs, insurance, maintenance. Explore your op-tions.

- Alternatives — Can you give up cable in favor of streaming services such as Netflix or Hulu? Can you use online options such as Skype to avoid big charges on your phone bill? Look for alternative options on your expenses. Borrow items instead of purchasing them. Utilize your local library. Split costs and share with friends and neighbors — anything from bulk paper goods to expensive lawn equipment. A little creativity can save you a lot of money.

Accumulating Savings

Whether it's for a special purchase or vacation, or just to have an emer-gency backup, having a savings account can be very useful.

If you're like me, you probably find that money disappears way too quickly. Between bills and everyday expenses, there just doesn't seem to be enough. So how can you have any hopes of putting some aside for long-term saving?

If money is tight, it's not easy. But there are some steps you can take to make it a little easier. Here are some ideas to get you started:

- Set up an automatic transfer from your checking account into a savings account. Treat it like a bill that has to get paid. When it's automatic, you have no choice but to put that money aside. Better yet, set up a cash reserve account at a separate institution, like Betterment. It will be slightly less accessible (so you're not tempted to spend it), plus have the added bonus of earning higher interest rates.

- Instead of paying with a debit or credit card, pay cash. And only pay with bills. Whenever you get coins, put them aside in a piggy bank. You'd be surprised how quickly change can add up, and you won't even notice.

- Some banks will let you set up your accounts so whenever you make a payment, the bank automatically rounds up and withdraws the whole dollar amount. The difference between the actual payment and the withdrawal amount goes into a savings account.

- When you go grocery shopping, pay with a debit card and get cash back. But instead of spending that cash, put it aside. It doesn't have to be a lot to add up quickly.

- Set a budget for purchases such as groceries or clothes. Then do your best to spend well under the budget. Put the difference in a savings account. You can even turn it into a game to see how much you can save!

There are countless other ways to save money, and the most important part is to find something that works for you. Trial and error can help. And you may find that you have to dip into your savings periodically if money is especially tight. Keep your eye on the long-term goal and don't beat yourself up over short-term setbacks. It will get easier, and saving will become second nature over time.

Chapter 5

GETTING OUT OF DEBT

I t is one of my dreams to be clear of debt. Perhaps it's one of your dreams, too. Unfortunately, I must admit that that dream is probably a long way from coming true. The realities of life have set me back. But I'm working on it! And making great progress. If you're in the same situation, with a mountain of debt staring you in the face each month, it's time to do something about it.

Without having much, if any, money at the end of the month, it's easier said than done. But there are still ways to bring that debt down. Here are a couple of ideas to help knock little chunks off the mountain. For more ideas, check out Chapter 4 on Saving Money:

- Cut back on living expenses — Our mortgage was locked in at 6.5% interest. It wasn't a horrible rate, and compared to many others, I'm sure it looks pretty decent. But since purchasing our home, interest rates had plummeted. Lower interest rates, combined with government programs put into place to help others who, like us, were struggling with increased property value as well as increased debt-to-income ratios, helped us refinance our house to lock in a new, lower 4% rate. Take a look at your living expenses. Are there areas that could get reduced? Could you get creative to lower those bills?

- "Bonus" money — Did you know that if you get paid weekly, but pay your bills monthly, you actually have enough to pay 13 months' worth of bills every year? Think about it: most months you'll get four paychecks for the months' expenses. But every three months you get a "bonus" check, giving you five checks for that month. If you continue to limit your expenses to four paychecks, that "bonus" check can be used to knock down debt. If you're looking to pay off credit card debt, student loans, etc., that money can make a huge dent in the amount you owe, saving you interest and stress. If you're looking to pay down a mortgage, some lenders will even let you work out an arrangement to pay every two weeks instead of once a month, so you automatically pay 13 months' worth of mortgage payments each year. That can save you tons of interest and have you owning your home free and clear a lot sooner.
  Along the same lines, when the time comes, if you get a tax refund, you can use that to pay down debt. Don't get a refund at the end of the year? Consider having a little bit more deducted from your paycheck each week. Not only will it save you the stress of having to scrounge up money to pay when tax time comes; it can also force you to save money. If you have difficulty saving money on your own, this forced "savings" plan may work out well for you.

If those ideas don't amount to enough, you can try some of the following options. While they don't reduce what you owe, they do ensure that more of what you pay each month goes toward the balance, not just interest:

- Balance transfers — Periodically credit card companies will offer their current customers (or prospective customers) balance transfer offers. If you have available credit (or good enough credit to open up a new account), you have the option of taking your existing debt and transferring it to this other account, usually at a reduced interest rate for a period of time. It can be a great option — if you have good credit and are able to pay off the debt before the promotional period ends. Keep in mind, however, that there are usually fees associated with balance transfers. Make sure those fees are less than you would be spending otherwise.

- Debt consolidation — Rather than owing to several different companies, you can combine all your debt and pay one company. Doing so may lower your interest rate and get you on a fixed payment plan that will actually pay off the debt. This can be done through a personal loan or through a debt consolidation company. Be sure to do your homework, however. There are plenty of companies out there ready to scam people who are looking for help. Research thoroughly any companies you think about dealing with.

- Ask for a lower rate — Depending on your credit score and history, you may be able to get a lower rate simply by asking for it. Contact your current lenders and ask to speak with someone who has authority when it comes to interest rate changes. Explain how you've been a valuable customer and you're looking to pay off your debt. They may be willing to work with you. You may also opt to close your account and set up a payment plan if your account is delinquent or on its way to collections. Sometimes, if the situation is bad enough, you may be able to work out a plan that has you paying only part of the debt, particularly if it's gone into collections.

Above all, try not to get discouraged. It can be very stressful to be in over your head, but taking a deep breath and working out a plan can be the best course of action for digging yourself out. It will take time, but you *will* get there.

Snowballs

You may have heard of a "snowball" method when it comes to paying down debt. Some financial gurus, particularly Dave Ramsey, promote this concept as a way to pay off your debt in a logical way that keeps you motivated. With the snowball method, if you have debt from multiple sources, you pay the minimum on all of the debts except the debt with the smallest balance. For the account with the smallest balance, you pay the minimum plus any extra you have to spend. This pays it off quickest, giving you a "win" for encouragement, and freeing up that monthly expense. Then you take what you were paying on that debt and apply that to the next smallest debt, so you're paying the minimum plus whatever extra you have. This clears up that debt next, giving you another win and freeing up more money that can be applied to the next smallest, and so on. By the time you get to the last debt, your payments are significantly higher on that one debt, paying it off quickly.

The concept is sound, but some critics argue that it doesn't take into account interest rates. If the debt with the highest balance also has the highest interest rate, are you saving money by applying extra payments to the smallest debt, or is any savings getting eaten up in interest?

To take an example from my own life, I currently have debt from multiple sources. One — the smallest debt — is on a store credit card. That debt also happens to have 0% interest for six months. If I were to pay off that one first, it would certainly improve cash flow, since I won't have that bill to pay each month, but I won't actually be saving money. As long as I pay enough to have that debt paid off before it starts accumulating interest, there's not much incentive to pay it off quickly. It would make more sense to use any extra money toward a debt that currently has interest being applied each month, since that would save me money.

It can certainly get very complicated and confusing, and it really boils down to what works best for you. If improving cash flow is priority, tackle the lowest debt. If you need a quick win to stay motivated, tackle the lowest debt. If you want to make the biggest impact on your bottom line, tackle the highest interest debt, regardless of where it falls on the balance list. Look at your finances and think about what makes the most sense for your personal situation.

Chapter 6

Extra Help

When it comes to money, you'll find a plethora of information out there, both online and in real life. Online resources, in particular, can be valuable tools. They can help with both general information and specific needs such as mortgage and retirement calculators. You can even get advice when it comes to your specific situation.

General Information

The sites below can offer general information on financial topics, as well as articles on the latest money and business news. Each site offers different categories, depending on your informational needs. Keep in mind that unless you're business or financially inclined, some of the terminology may be advanced, requiring additional research. If you're less technically inclined, check out the last site, Dow Janes, for simpler, easier-to-understand guidance:

- MSN: https://www.msn.com/en-us/money

- Dow Jones: https://www.dowjones.com/smartmoney/

- AARP: https://www.aarp.org/money/

- Dow Janes: https://www.dowjanes.com/free-resources

The great thing about these sites is that whether you're looking for personal financial information or information for your business's finances, resources are available. So no matter what your goals are, you can get the help and information you need.

Calculators

Depending on your goal, you may be wondering what you have to do to meet your end result. Luckily there are many resources out there that suit this exact purpose, with calculators for mortgages, retirement, auto loans, of any of hundreds of other financial goals. Below are a couple of sites with several options, but there are many others out there, as well. If you're looking for a specific type of calculator, try searching online.

- CNN's financial calculators: https://www.cnn.com/business/financial-calculators

- Practical Money Skills's calculators: https://www.practicalmoneyskills.com/en/resources/financial-calculators.html

Other Resources

Experts and other consumers can often help with specific questions or issues, and they share their knowledge in a variety of ways, such as forums and podcasts. Below are a few options to get you started. You can also search for forums online by searching for "forum: topic" or search for podcasts through your favorite podcast platform.

- Forum on Money Saving Expert: https://forums.moneysavingexpert.com/

- Personal finance podcasts:

  - Smart Money by NerdWallet

- The Ramsey Show

- The Clark Howard Podcast

- Smart Passive Income

This is just the beginning. Magazines, smart phone apps, books, radio shows, YouTube channels, and more offer advice, opinions, and guidance on any financial topic you can think of, often for free. Think about where you want to be, and find the best guides to help you get there.

Part Three

CAREER

Chapter 1

GETTING STARTED

Maybe you're miserable in your current job. Maybe you just feel like you're getting nowhere. Or maybe you don't even know what you want to do, so you find yourself in a meaningless job to make ends meet until you figure it out. Whatever the reason, your career could use a facelift. And you've decided to take charge and make it happen. Unfortunately, now comes the hard part: how are you going to change it?

If you don't know where to start, I hope this section will point you in the right direction. You'll find guidance on:

- Figuring out what you want to do

- How to get the skills and experience you need

- Finding the right job (even if it's not a "normal" 9-5 job)

- Where to get extra help

It won't be an easy journey, but you'll learn a lot about yourself, about what you want, and about how to get where you want to be.

If you're panicking a bit about the process, take a deep breath. I read somewhere that the average person has three or four careers in his or her lifetime. Not jobs, *careers*. So you're not locked into one thing for the rest of your life unless you want to be. If something sounds interesting, give it a shot. If you like it, put more time and money and effort into it. If it's not your thing, keep searching.

Now I'm not condoning job hopping. That won't really help you. But if you find something that sounds good, read a little about it, search job postings, and talk to others in the field. If it still sounds like something you'd be interested in, pursue it. If not, look elsewhere. It's your life, and your career. The ultimate choice is yours. So let's begin, shall we?

Chapter 2

WHAT DO YOU WANT TO DO?

I f your mind is thinking "aaahh!!" to that question, then you're not alone. I had a lot of those moments. I did personality tests online; I browsed job postings; I read books — anything to try and come up with "the perfect job." It wasn't easy.

The trouble for me was: I had lots of interests, but nothing really stood out to me when it came to determining my life's work. Even when I came up with what I thought was the perfect solution, an obvious choice that met my criteria, I encountered an obstacle in the form of low income. I wanted to be a writer, and I still do, but I knew that getting to the point where I made enough income to support myself would be challenging and lengthy. Since I was facing divorce and knew I would need reliable, steady income to support myself and my kids, I had to keep looking. I knew I wouldn't be satisfied with "just a job." Fortunately, with more soul-searching and research, I found a well-paying career that would give me what I needed and wanted.

For you, the choice may be easier, even if the execution isn't. Perhaps you know what you've always wanted to do but lack the education or experience to get there. Perhaps you have an interest but don't know how to turn it into a career. Or perhaps you're in the same boat I was in. I knew I didn't want just another job. I wanted something that was meaningful to me, that I would enjoy, that I could see myself doing for years, that wouldn't bore me. I just didn't know what.

Your criteria may be different. Perhaps you're not as picky as I was (for your sake, I hope you aren't!) and will have better luck finding something that "clicks" for you. Perhaps you have a few career paths that interest you and you're just trying to narrow them down. Perhaps you've got some ideas floating around in your mind. Or perhaps you have no idea where to even start. No matter what's been holding you back, it's time to figure out what you want.

What's Important to You?

Before even thinking about which career path to choose, take a few moments to think about what's really important to you. What qualities are you looking for in a job? Are you looking for something with a consistent schedule, steady paycheck, and great benefits? Are you looking for something that lets you think creatively, coming up with ideas that are "outside the box" on a regular basis? Do you want to work with other people or independently? In a large corporation or mom-and-pop operation?

The questions are endless, but only you can really answer them. Only you will know what's important to you, what will make you happy. If you relish working independently but find yourself in a job that requires you to be part of a team, would you be okay with that? If you need the security of a steady paycheck but find yourself drawn to a commission-only profession, how will you deal with that?

Taking the time to really evaluate these criteria — before you fall in love with a job that won't work for you — will help ensure you find a career that is truly the best fit.

Getting Ideas

Once you know what's important to you, it's time to start exploring your options. Whether you have an idea of what you might want to do or not, getting a feel for what's out there will help you be sure of your choice.

To get started, think about things that interest you. What kind of hobbies could you see yourself doing full time? Is there something you love reading about, learning more about, seeing in action? What did you want to be when you grew up? Reconnecting with that part of yourself can give you a glimpse into your subconscious.

I found one interesting way to get ideas was to take personality tests. You answer a bunch of questions, and your answers are interpreted to give you an idea of which category your personality falls into. Included in the results are usually famous people who had your personality type and some career ideas that may appeal to you. Using these tests as a starting point may inspire you and lead you into a direction you hadn't even considered. Below are some online tests to get you started:

- Quest Career Services: https://questcareer.com/career-test/

- 123 Test: https://www.123test.com/career-test/

- O-Net Interest Profiler: https://www.mynextmove.org/explore/ip

- Truity: https://www.truity.com/view/tests/personality-career

Tests aren't the only way to brainstorm career ideas. Think about hobbies or interests you have and visit online job search sites, such as CareerBuilder. Type your hobby or interest in the keyword search box and see what comes up. The jobs don't even have to be local; you're just brainstorming here. Or you can do an internet search with your hobby or interest and "job" or "career" to see what comes up.

Another option is mind-mapping. Take a blank piece of paper. In the middle of the paper write a hobby, interest, or job characteristic that's important to you. Circle it. Now draw a line from that circle and write a word that relates to it in some way. It can be a job idea or just another interest, job characteristic, or random thought. Circle that, too. Continue to branch off the circles, both the original circle and the ones you create as you go. See where your mind takes you. You might be surprised at the chain of ideas!

Stay True to Yourself

If you come up with a possible career, but keep searching for excuses why it wouldn't work, ask yourself why. When I came up with my original choice, I fought it. I knew it wouldn't be an easy path. Aside from the unreliable paycheck that ultimately became a dealbreaker, I would have to constantly use my brain, my creativity to push myself forward. I would be consistently challenged, needing to learn and problem solve and try new things. But the more I thought about it, the more I realized that those things that I was fighting were actually the parts that made it right for me. I relished challenge, and jobs that were steady and reliable also tended to bore me. The "normal" job had never been the best choice for me. And even though I had to find something else to keep a roof over my head, I'm still working on that first choice as a side gig. I haven't given it up, because it's that important to me. It's a part of me.

It's important to keep in mind that what's right for you may not be easy or straightforward. But to find the job that's truly right for you, you need to do some soul-searching. You need to think about what you enjoy doing, what challenges you, what gets you excited, what stirs your blood. It's about bringing together what's important to you and what's interesting to you. Even if the path to get there won't be easy — or if you have to combine it with something else to get all your needs met — if it's something that's meaningful for you, the end result will be more than worth it.

It may take a while to discover the right career for you. You may have a few false starts. But stick with it. The process will lead you to the right choice.

Chapter 3

GETTING THE SKILLS YOU NEED

Once you've figured out what it is you want to do, it's time to figure out what's keeping you from getting there. What do you need to get where you want to be?

Education

The new career I settled on, becoming a librarian, required a specialized Masters Degree. Not ideal as a new single parent, but I knew it would benefit me in the long run. So I did my research, found a program that wouldn't cost an arm and a leg but was also reputable, completely online, and could be completed within a couple of years. Then I took the plunge.

If education is the hang-up for you, the good news is that the wide variety of educational and financial aid programs make it possible for just about anyone to get a degree. It may take a while, depending on your available time and support system, but it's possible. Think about what kind of program would work out best for you and do some research.

You're likely bombarded on a regular basis with ads for colleges, citing that now is the best time to go back to school and earn your degree. And it's true: education can give you a boost, whether it's in your current field or in a new one. But before you start applying to colleges, think about all your options first.

College Degrees

Depending on the field you're looking at, it's a somewhat unfortunate fact that many employers won't even look at your resume unless you've got a degree, regardless of what that degree is in. If you don't have one, even if you're qualified for the position, you may be passed over. Research the field you're looking to break into and see if a degree is a required or even preferred qualification. Even if a bachelor's or associate's degree isn't required, some fields will require certification programs as a prerequisite for employment.

Keep in mind, however, that even if you *do* need to get a degree, it likely doesn't need to be from an Ivy League school to be an asset. Local schools are excellent options, as are accredited online universities. Evaluate your time and your finances and determine the best course of action for you. And don't worry if you can't afford to get that degree. If it's important to you, there are many financial aid programs available. Or you may be able to find a roundabout way to break into that field.

Continuing Education

If you already have a degree, or don't need one in your chosen field, you can still benefit from education. Taking a class or two at a local college or online can make you an asset in your current and future positions. You gain valuable knowledge, and you show your employer that you're serious about improving yourself (definitely a selling point when you're looking for that promotion or raise). Check with your current employer; they may even offer reimbursement for education.

In addition to college courses, many towns offer continuing education programs that can teach you skills in life or your career. You can also participate in seminars on leadership, time management, and more. The more you learn, the better off you'll be. Even if the course or seminar isn't directly related to what you're currently doing or what you hope to do in the future, you can still gain valuable skills. And don't discount the valuable networking possibilities, as well. Courses and seminars can be a great way to meet people in different fields — people who can be a foot in the door for future opportunities.

Experience

It can be a bit of a conundrum to look at job postings; everyone wants experienced workers, but you can't get experience without getting a job — right? Maybe not.

Internships

If you're still in school or recently graduated, you can look for internship opportunities. Some may be paid, but even if they aren't, you'll gain the experience necessary to put on your resume and get real-world application of your skills. Depending on where you intern, you may even be able to get a job after the internship is over. Or, at the very least, gain valuable contacts that can help you find another position.

Contact local employers and organizations to see if it's possible to intern with them. Some companies will also advertise internships through their websites or through job sites, like CareerBuilder.

Volunteer

Another option is to look into volunteering at non-profit organizations. Many smaller groups and organizations don't have the funds to hire a professional. You can volunteer to do the job for a nominal fee, or for free. They get the job done, and you gain experience. Regardless of what you need experience in, there is likely an organization who could use the help. Check out sites like the ones below to get you started:

- VolunteerMatch: https://www.volunteermatch.org/

- AmeriCorps: https://americorps.gov/partner/communities-initiatives/united-we-serve

- Great Nonprofits: https://greatnonprofits.org/

Spread the Word

Don't underestimate the power of friends and family. Let them know you're looking for experience. Perhaps someone knows a person who could hire you. Or perhaps a friend or member of your family could use help themselves. As with an organization, even if you're not charging much — if anything — you'll still gain that valuable experience you need.

And don't forget the option of going out on your own. Advertise your services in the local paper or online. Be upfront and honest about looking for experience. Many people are willing to take a chance if it'll be a lot cheaper for them. It's a win-win.

Connections

In some fields, in particular, it seems as if you can't get anywhere without knowing someone. But if you're new to the field and don't know anyone who works in it, how do you break in?

Go Online

To start, read all you can about the field and talk with others who've started and succeeded in that field. The internet can be a valuable resource when it comes to finding opportunities and individuals in a specific field. Join forums, participate in discussions, and absorb as much information as you can. You never know who you'll connect with, or what opportunities they may present.

Spread the Word

As with getting experience, don't forget to spread the word when it comes to starting a new career. Someone may know someone who knows someone — and that last someone can be your foot in the door. Even if the people you know can't help by way of introducing you to people, they may present opportunities to get involved, and that can lead to new contacts and opportunities.

Network

Join your local chamber of commerce to meet others in your area and connect with people in your chosen field. They can be a fountain of knowledge when it comes to getting experience, learning what to do next, and meeting even more people who can help you. You can also try joining organizations for your chosen field to network with others. Or look for lectures, seminars, and conferences conducted by people you admire in the field. A little research can go a long way.

Don't Be Shy

When you meet new people, don't be afraid to express your interest in a particular area. I wouldn't recommend introducing yourself as "Hi, I'm Joe. I'm looking for a job in marketing" unless you're at a career expo, but bringing up the industry or topic in conversation can lead to some interesting responses. You never know who you'll meet or what that person might be able to do for you. (While you're at it, keep your ears and eyes open for opportunities that may help others. Networking is a two-way street, and just as someone you meet may be able to give your career a boost, you or someone you know can offer the same benefits to someone else.)

Gaps in Employment

If you find yourself relatively unemployable due to gaps in employment — particularly if you've been out of work for any length of time due to a lay-off or personal issues — you may need something temporary so the gap doesn't widen. Ideally, this something will be related to your chosen field, but it doesn't have to be if you can still explain how the opportunity made you grow and learn new skills.

Gaps can be filled with internships, volunteer opportunities, or education, as described above, but you can also look for a temporary job.

To find these temporary positions, you can partner with an employment agency, ask friends and family, or simply check out job listings. Many companies seek out extra workers to help them get through busy seasons, or they may be looking for someone to cover a vacation, maternity leave, or sabbatical.

Depending on your availability, options may be limited. But chances are pretty high that you can find something that will work with whatever obligations or skill set you may have. Here are some ideas to get you started:

- Retail (particularly seasonal positions)

- Landscaping

- Construction

- Computer/technical assistance

- Office assistance

- Odd jobs (i.e. painting, garage cleaning, gutter cleaning, etc.)

- Babysitting, house-sitting, pet-sitting

- Delivering newspapers or food orders

- Lifeguarding

Many more specific positions will have openings, as well. To get more information on those opportunities, look for specialized employment agencies or browse job boards online.

Chapter 4

FINDING THE RIGHT JOB

The biggest part of changing your career is finding a position in the new career you've chosen. The same applies if you're switching jobs or employers. You have many options when it comes to looking for a job, and the one that works best for you will likely be determined by your chosen profession. Here are some tips to get you started.

Online

The quickest and easiest way to search for jobs currently is on the World Wide Web. Log on to the internet, and you'll find countless sites that claim to have the best listings for your area and profession. In addition to available jobs, many now offer career services, with everything from resume building to information about trends and salary expectations.

CareerBuilder (https://www.careerbuilder.com/)

CareerBuilder is one of the largest online job sites in the U.S., especially now that it has merged with Monster. Easy to use, with a huge selection of postings across the country, CareerBuilder.com is for many the first choice. For job seekers, search results can be narrowed by location, salary, and more, making it possible to narrow down exactly the type of job you're looking for. After a resume is submitted, CareerBuilder will also present a list of recommended jobs based on previous searches or application history, and they will send out emails with recommendations, as well.

Indeed (https://www.indeed.com/)

Indeed is another great choice for overall searching and browsing. Search for your criteria, and it brings up pages of jobs. Or browse listings to see which jobs match qualifications on your linked resume. You can also customize your profile to specify qualifications, job preferences, and search criteria, personalizing your job search.

SnagAJob (https://www.snagajob.com/)

Though not as well known, SnagAJob offers many postings from reputable companies. Simple, easy to use, its focus appears to be blue collar, hourly employment, though it does also have listings for other careers, as well. As with other sites, it offers tips and guidance to job seekers entering the workforce.

Ladders (https://www.theladders.com/)

On the opposite end of the spectrum is Ladders, which gears itself toward high-end positions with salaries over $100K. Though some job listings are below that salary, positions mainly consist of upper management, executive, and director jobs that require extensive experience.

Industry Specific Website and Non-Traditional Jobs

For more specific listings that focus on the desired position or industry, try browsing job sites that are designed for that purpose. Some professional organizations will also feature job sections that highlight current openings. Search online using the desired career and "jobs" to see what comes up.

Newspapers

Though not nearly as prevalent as they used to be, classified listings in newspapers can still be a useful tool for job searchers, especially for those looking at local, small-scale jobs in small offices or companies. If you don't subscribe to local papers, you can check with your local library to see if they subscribe, or head to the newspaper's website to find listings.

Employment Agencies

Many larger companies who don't want to deal with the hassle of finding prospective employees hire employment agencies to do the searching for them. These employment agencies can be small, serving a specific county, or nationwide, even international.

Listings of employment agencies can be found online, or you can browse job postings to find jobs posted by employment agencies. Applying for a job that's posted by an employment agency can help get your foot in the door, by making that agency familiar with your resume and the type of job you're looking for. Some agencies will also have open houses, during which they will actively seek new employees to work with their agencies.

Positions available through agencies can be temporary, temp-to-hire, or direct hire. Temporary, as their name suggests, are not permanent positions. They can be anything from a single week to long-term for a year or more. Temp-to-hire positions start as temporary positions, and if the employer feels you are a good match, that employer can make a job offer. Direct hire positions are regular, permanent positions that are being filled.

Employment agencies vary widely and can be general or specialized in a particular industry. If you are looking for positions in a specific field, matching up with an employment agency that works with that field can help get you experience and contacts, even if just for temporary positions to boost your resume.

Career Expos and Job Fairs

Occasionally companies will get together to attract job seekers. These fairs, usually sponsored by members of the media or event planning companies, will draw an assortment of industries and positions. Employers are looking to speak with prospects on the spot, to answer questions, accept resumes, and set up the next steps in the process.

Attending an event can be beneficial if you have an interest in some or all of the companies that will be present. Be prepared with several copies of your resume, and dress to impress. You'll also want to be prepared in the event an employer wants to interview you then and there.

Career expos and job fairs are usually well-advertised in newspapers, online, and on job boards.

Cold Calls

Another option is to simply call prospective employers and ask if they have any openings. Jobs that are recently available, or are not advertised, may be made known to those answering the phone. Asking may be the quickest, or even only, way to find out about these jobs.

Not all companies look favorably to cold calls, however, so always be polite and don't burn bridges you may need down the line.

Networking

Perhaps the oldest way of finding a job can also be the most effective: knowing someone. Whether that person is a close friend or family member, or a friend of a friend of a friend, having a link with someone who works at a prospective employer is a definite benefit, as long as that person is willing to help you get a foot in the door.

When you're looking for a job, make everyone you know aware of what you're looking for. You never know who might have a valuable connection.

Getting Hired

Once you've applied to potential jobs, you will likely (hopefully!) get called in for interviews. Most interviews will take place face-to-face, but an initial interview or an interview for a position a long distance from your current residence may take place virtually or over the phone instead.

Here are some overall tips to make a good impression during an interview:

- Dress to impress — If the interview is for a professional position, wear a suit. If this position is more casual, dress a little nicer than the position calls for: wear nice slacks or a skirt, and a clean dress shirt, polo, blouse, or sweater. No jeans and no t-shirts. Make sure your clothes are clean and wrinkle-free and that your hair is neat. Show the interviewer that you care about your appearance and are serious about the position. First impressions count.

- Be present — Make eye contact and show the interviewer that you're interested in what he or she is saying. Avoiding eye contact or acting distracted can indicate that you're hiding something or are just not really interested in being there.

- Be alert — Don't slouch or lean back in a relaxed, reclined position. Sit up straight. Act professional. Acknowledge what the interviewer is saying.

- Be confident in your answers — This shows that you're confident in yourself, as well.

- Elaborate — Don't answer questions with a simple "yes" or "no," unless that's what the question calls for. Explain to the interviewer what you bring to the table, and why you're the best person for the position.

- Don't make excuses — Many of us have areas on our resumes that are detours from our career path or that we're not necessarily proud of. Don't make excuses for them or apologize for them. Instead, explain how you've learned from those experiences and used each item to your benefit.

- Be honest — Telling "white lies" may get you through the interview, but if you're hired, you'll soon be discovered. Be honest with yourself and the interviewer. If you can't do the job, or you're missing a necessary skill, lying about it won't help you in the long run.

- Be respectful — Greet your interviewer with a handshake. Thank the interviewer for his or her time. Don't interrupt or ignore the interviewer when he or she is talking. Show the interviewer that you are professional, courteous, and can treat others with the respect they deserve.

If you find yourself being interviewed by phone, many of the same tips apply. Obviously the interviewer can't see how you're dressed, but you will still want to be honest, respectful, and confident. Elaborate on your answers, really listen to what the interviewer is saying, and thank the interviewer for his or her time.

Common Interview Questions

- What are your strengths? What are your weaknesses, or areas in which you could improve?

An employer wants to know how the company will benefit from hiring you. What are you capable of? How will you fill the position? On the flip side, knowing not only where your talents lie, but also where you can improve, shows that you are aware of your limitations and are not afraid to work on improving them.

- Where do you see yourself in 5 or 10 years?
  This tells the interviewer what your goals are, and whether employment in the open position could be a permanent position in the company, or a temporary stop for you in your travels. This also shows the interviewer that you can plan ahead, and that you're motivated to move beyond your current situation. Explaining how you want to better yourself will show that you are going places. Don't be afraid to mention personal goals, in addition to career goals. Employers want well-rounded associates.

- Tell me about yourself.
  Though not technically a question, be prepared to tell the interviewer a little about yourself. This doesn't mean start at birth and work your way up. Rather, tell the interviewer about your work history, what you offer, and what you're looking for. If you have extracurricular activities that can be considered an asset, mention those as well. If you have a family, now would be a good time to mention them if relevant. Any lapses in employment, items on your resume that need explanation, or items that may affect your employment status should also be mentioned.

- Do you have any questions for me?
  This is a tricky question, and depending on how the interview has gone so far, you may not have any questions for the interviewer. But asking at least one intelligent question in return will show the interviewer that you were paying attention, and that you're actually interested in the position. Try asking for an elaboration on something the interviewer touched on, or specific questions about the open position. While inquiring about salary or benefits is okay, don't dwell too much on these

— the employer may think you're only interested in the money, not the job itself.

Chapter 5

NOT A 9-5

Many people are content with a "regular" job — punching in and out every day, getting a paycheck from "the man." But if you're one of the many who want something different in a career, you may be wondering what to do, where to start, and how to advance. Rest assured you're not alone, and there are plenty of people and resources out there to help you.

Work From Home

Working from home is becoming increasingly popular, and there are several different formats that can fall under this category. You may own your own business, work for someone else but determine your own schedule, or work for someone else on a set schedule. Some jobs from home will require conference calls or regular reports in, while other jobs will just require completed projects or tasks. You may even get a job working from home that requires a separate phone line and computer system for the job — and you answer customer calls and act as someone in an office would.

If you'd like to work at home as an independent contractor with your own business, you can post your services online at sites such as Upwork (https://www.upwork.com/). To find a position with a particular company, you can do an online search through job sites or general search sites, or you can contact companies directly and ask if they hire work-at-home employees. If you already have a job and would like to bring it home, ask your employer about the possibility.

Creative Jobs

Actors, dancers, artists, writers — if you're creative, your talents may not lead to a "normal" job. You may be hired for particular projects or jobs rather than ongoing employment. You may choose to be associated with an organization or agent that can get you jobs, or you can go out on your own and make a mark. It's not an easy path, but if you've got the passion, you can certainly succeed. The toughest part will be getting your name out there so you can get clients and jobs. Be sure to advertise and, if appropriate, join professional organizations that can help you on your path. Look into marketing. And as with so many other things, networking can definitely be your friend.

Independent Representatives — Multi-Level Marketing

You're likely familiar with companies that involve independent representatives: Scentsy, Tula XII, Stella & Dot, etc. You can ask others you know who are involved with these companies or visit the companies' websites to get more information on how to join.

Being an independent representative is, essentially, owning your own business (so check out the next section, too). However, there are some differences. You'll be affiliated with an existing, established company — a company that may supplement or fund your salary. And there will likely be a set structure in place that determines how much you make, how you can progress and advance, and what you will sell or promote. The good part is that you control your success. You can go as far as you want, and you determine your own schedule. Keep in mind, however, that these arrangements usually involve a start-up cost, as well as possible inventory and supply costs, plus ongoing costs such as maintaining a website. And they require constant hustle, selling items to potential customers.

Starting Your Own Business

If your dream is to have your own business, welcome to the club! While there is a lot to consider, many have gone before you and succeeded.

Entrepreneurs tend to have many similar traits that serve them well in their careers. Among these traits are: a drive to succeed, the ability to self-motivate, creativity, and a willingness to think "outside the box." If you're missing some or all of these qualities, you can still successfully run your own business, but the journey may be a bit more difficult. Having the passion for what you decide to do, however, can outweigh just about anything. You can hire others to fill in the gaps if it comes to that.

If you decide that starting a business is the right choice for you, you'll next need to decide what it is you want to do. This can be based on a talent or a passion or both, but make sure whatever you decide holds your interest enough that you're willing to stick with it in the long term. If you lose interest after a short while, your business is not likely to succeed. Passion for what you're doing can keep you going, but lack of passion can dwindle your chances of success.

Another thing to keep in mind is the money factor. Regardless of what you decide to do, chances are pretty slim that you'll bring in a lot of money right off the bat. You need to be mentally and physically prepared for the lack of funds in the beginning. There will be a lot of expenses and not much income, and you'll still have living expenses not related to the business, as well. Think about cutting back or building your savings — or, ideally, both — before making the business your primary source of income.

Here are some questions to ask yourself to get started:

- What will you do?

- Will you work by yourself, or will you need partners or employees?

- How will you get paid?

- Where will start-up money come from? Will you need a loan?

- Will you work out of your home, or will you need a physical location? How will you pay for the associated expenses?

- How will you let the world know about your business? Who is your clientele?

- How will you deal with customer/client concerns?

This is by no means an exhaustive list, and you'll likely keep adding to it as you go. You don't need to have all the answers right away, but the more research and preparation you can do beforehand, the more likely you are to be successful. Many have gone before you, but success it not guaranteed. Think long and hard about your choices and the path you want to take. And good luck! Owning your business is not easy.

To get more advice or assistance with starting your own business, including information about creating a business plan, check out the U.S. Small Business Association (https://www.sba.gov/) and SCORE (https://www.score.org/).

Chapter 6

Extra Help

Whether you're looking for ideas, applying for jobs, or looking for assistance with resumes, interview strategies, and more, the internet is a valuable tool. We've already discussed a few sites that can help you with your career path. Here are some of them again, as well as a few other sites that can help.

Job Search

When it comes to searching for jobs themselves, many sites will offer listings of available jobs, especially if it relates somewhat to the site's content. The largest number of jobs, however, can be found on the larger, general job-posting sites. Check out:

- CareerBuilder (https://www.careerbuilder.com/)

- Indeed (https://www.indeed.com/)

If you have a specific industry or area you want to work in, search for industry-specific or location-specific sites that can offer more specialized search tools and resources.

General Information

In addition to job listings, the sites above offer additional resources, such as articles on resume writing and interview skills, that can provide information and guidance in your search. Other sites also offer information in these areas and more. Here are some to get you started:

- Career One Stop (https://www.careeronestop.org/)

- U.S. Bureau of Labor Statistics (https://www.bls.gov/ooh/)

- CollegeGrad (https://collegegrad.com/careers/all)

Forums

Forums can be helpful, especially when it comes to specific questions or up-to-the-minute updates and information. You can search for forums regarding a specific topic or industry by heading to your favorite search engine and searching for "forum: topic or industry." Below are some general career forums to get you started:

- Career Village (https://www.careervillage.org/)

- Job Stars (https://jobstars.com/career-blogs-forums/)

- GlassDoor (https://www.glassdoor.com/Community/index.htm)

Forums can also offer support and feedback in your career path and overall career goals — as well as the all-important networking. This is especially useful if you're feeling isolated in your journey or feel that others around you don't understand what you're going through.

Other Resources

In addition to websites and forums, there are other tools that can offer help and inspiration. Some local libraries will offer access to specialized databases or platforms to help job seekers. You can also check out podcasts, blogs, newspapers, magazines, apps, and more. Search the web or through your device's app store to get ideas.

Part Four

HEALTH

Chapter 1

Getting Started

When it comes to your health, there are some things you have control over, and some things you don't. I'm sure if we could all live a healthy, pain-free life, we would. Unfortunately it doesn't work that way. But that doesn't mean you can't take charge to tackle health issues you're facing. This section will get you started with some tips, suggestions, and ideas.

Taking charge of your health, though, is more than just tackling the weight issue or the quitting smoking issue — or any of the more specific, demanding goals you've established. Taking care of your health is about making sure you're running your best, keeping yourself in shape and healthy. Need convincing? Here are some reasons why making your health a priority can be a good thing:

- You'll feel better

- You'll look better

- You'll catch problems earlier — which means a better chance of recovery

- You'll have lower overall medical bills, because you'll have less issues less often

First Things First

If you're convinced that taking overall care of yourself is the best course of action, there's no time like the present to start. Schedule a physical with your primary care physician (PCP) to get checked out. Women, also schedule an exam with your gynecologist. Don't have a PCP or gynecologist? Check your insurance company's provider director or try the sites below to find a provider:

- WebMD: https://doctor.webmd.com/

- HealthGrades: https://www.healthgrades.com/find-a-doctor

- Zocdoc: https://book.zocdoc.com/get-started

While you're at it, schedule a check-up with your dentist and optometrist, too. Get everything checked out so you know what you're working with. To find a dentist or optometrist, try the sites below:

- EveryDentist: https://www.everydentist.com/

- Dentists.com: https://dentists.com/

- American Optometric Association: https://www.aoa.org/

Once you've made your appointments, take a few minutes to think about anything you may want to discuss with the doctors. Are there any concerns you have? Questions you have? Have you noticed anything "off" about your body lately? Any symptoms you can't quite explain? Write down anything you want to know more about or want the doctor to check out.

Now here's the key: take that list and actually talk to the doctor. It can be easy to get shy or nervous when talking about personal, private things like your body. But the doctor can't help unless he or she knows what's wrong. And that doctor won't know how you feel. Try not to be nervous — there's likely nothing you can say or feel that the doctor hasn't dealt with before. Think how much better you'll feel just getting reassurance or taking measures to get well!

Take notes during the appointments if necessary. What is the doctor recommending you do? Are there vitamins or medications he or she is recommending? An exercise regimen to start or continue? Special diet to follow? Are there tests he or she is sending you for? Anything you need to monitor? If you don't agree with something or have concerns about it, get a second opinion.

Once the appointments are over, though, you're not done. It's one thing to go to the doctor and get checked out. It's quite another to follow through and actually carry out the recommendations the doctor has made. To get yourself in tip-top shape and keep yourself there, you need to take into consideration what the doctor has recommended. Now that you know what you're dealing with, it's time to come up with a game plan.

Game Plans

When it comes to taking charge of your health, there is a lot of trial and error. It can be hard to determine in the beginning what will work for you. You may start with the best of intentions and decide to tackle a strict diet and exercise routine only to find that you're constantly "cheating" and not sticking with it. To come up with a game plan, gather up all the knowledge you've gained thus far and figure out where to go from here.

- Are you working on getting a disease or disorder under control? Are there specific steps that must be taken?

- Is there something your doctor has indicated you must do to get healthy? (i.e. cut back on fatty foods to help your cholesterol)

- What are your ultimate goals? What steps must reasonably be taken to get there?

- What kind of diet restrictions do you have? How healthy can you make your diet over the long-term?

- What kind of fitness regimen works best for you? What will you be able to stick with long-term?

The key to this is longevity — both in game plan and in life. The reason so many diets fail is because they're not sustainable. It's not likely you'll be able to give up all your favorite foods for the rest of your life. But finding a diet that works for your personality and lifestyle while considering your restrictions can help you make better choices and stay healthy long-term. And the same applies to most health choices: exercise, getting professional help, relieving stress, etc. Unless something is truly a matter of life and death, you have flexibility in determining what you'll do to improve and what lifestyle changes you'll make. Sometimes you'll need to be tough with yourself; sometimes you can be a bit more lenient. Remember your doctor's recommendations and proceed accordingly.

So what works? Upon evaluating your trials and errors over the past several months (or years!), what have you found that works for you? Are there changes you can live with and stick with for the foreseeable future? Determine what these changes are and how you'll incorporate them into your life.

Once you have a course of action, stick with it. It won't always be easy, especially if the changes are drastic. And you won't feel brand new right away. These things take time. Just take them one step at a time and keep your eye on the ultimate goal of being healthy. And think about how great you'll feel as you get there.

Remember: nothing is set in stone. If you find something doesn't work, or you want to try something different, you can make adjustments accordingly. Just keep in mind that if the ultimate goal here is to get healthy and live longer, you want to be able to tolerate the choices that you'll be living with — because you'll be living with them for a while!

Chapter 2

DIET

When you think about diets, chances are the first thing that comes to mind is losing weight. Atkins, South Beach, Slim Fast specific diets designed to make you lose weight fast. But diets are about so much more than shedding pounds.

The food you consume plays a huge role in your life. It can affect not only your weight, but your energy levels, your risks of getting certain diseases, and your overall wellbeing, as well. Having a well-balanced diet can help you lower your weight, yes, but it can also just plain make you feel good.

Your dietary needs and limitations can adjust the specifics of what you can and cannot eat, and to determine the best diet for your individual needs, I encourage you to speak with your medical practitioners. In general, the goal is to fill your diet with a variety of proteins, whole grains, fruits, and vegetables, and to limit sugar and fat intake. You've likely heard basic guidelines since you were in elementary school, and your personality may make staying within the guidelines easy or difficult. Keep in mind that you can control what you eat, however, and you can take charge of this part of your life, just as you can with the others.

Planning ahead can be your best tool when it comes to revamping your diet and filling your body with wholesome meals and snacks. Try making as many of your own meals as possible. This will help you avoid preservatives and processing that may negate some of the nutritional qualities present in your food. Plan your menu in advance so you have all the necessary ingredients to put together a balanced meal. Prepare snacks ahead of time so you're not scurrying to the vending machine or convenience store when a craving strikes.

When you're evaluating your diet, keep in mind that even something that's nutritious won't offer everything you need. You have to balance proteins, carbohydrates, fruits, and vegetables. Start with meals that offer lean protein in the form of meat, eggs, tofu, or beans. Add whole grains such as brown rice or whole wheat pasta. Finish off with a salad or other vegetables — the brighter, bolder the colors, the better. When it comes to snacks, look for treats that offer nutritional value. If possible, get snacks that offer protein, as well, to keep you feeling full longer. Some suggestions: apple slices or celery sticks with peanut butter, veggies dipped in hummus, plain yogurt with fruit or granola mixed in.

Be on the lookout for empty calories. Sweets, salty snacks, and processed foods are all high in not-so-good-for-you ingredients. They may fill you up, but they won't give your body the nutrients it needs. And your body responds to sugar and artificial sweeteners like a drug — it craves more, leaving you feeling hungry, cranky, and reaching for more empty calories. And don't forget what you drink. Sometimes that can play just as big a role as food. Reach for water whenever possible, forgoing sugary soft drinks.

Speaking of water, drink it! And drink *lots* of it. A huge portion of our bodies is made up of water, and we need it to keep functioning at peak efficiency. Don't wait to get thirsty; drink periodically throughout the day. Keep a glass or bottle at your desk, in your car, with every snack or meal. You'd be amazed what a little water can do.

Fighting Temptation

I am of the mindset that you shouldn't deprive yourself. If you truly want something, forcing yourself not to have it often has the opposite effect than you desire: you want it even more, and eventually go on a binge, resulting in more consumed calories than if you had simply had a small portion of the item you desired in the first place. That being said, going crazy and eating everything that looks or sounds good isn't the right course of action, either. You need to evaluate what you want most and focus on portion control: a single cookie instead of a plateful, a small slice of pie or cake, a lone pastry. Satisfy the craving and move on.

Certain times of year, such as during the holidays, birthdays, or summer barbecue season, it may seem that your well-balanced diet is in jeopardy. Going overboard is far too easy when confronted with a plethora of treats and goodies. How can you stay on track?

Despite the overabundance of treats, meals often also have assorted not-as-bad-for-you options. Look for lean means and salads and other simple vegetables (not candied, casseroled, or dripping with butter!) Herbs and spices aren't bad for you, so go for options with those rather than sauces. Avoid filling up with breads and sweetened sides, which are filled with empty calories.

Another method is to eat before you go to special events. Fill up with a healthy snack or meal before you go to that party, and you won't be as tempted to grab everything you see. You'll already be pretty full, so you'll only have a small portion of whatever looks best.

The most important thing is to keep your eye on the prize. Remember why you're trying to lose that weight or get healthy. Is having another cookie worth faltering in that goal? Take action to remind yourself every time you go to reach for something. Keep a note or picture in your pocket, so you can pull it out periodically as a reminder. Or if there's someone with you who knows about your goals, have that person be your conscience and tap the back of your hand every time you try to grab something you shouldn't.

Another technique is simply to distract yourself. Focusing on food is easy when you're bored or have nothing else to think about or do. Distract yourself with a task, person, or activity you have interest in. Get your mind off the food, and you'll forget to grab that fatty treat.

Chapter 3

Exercise

Most doctors will tell you that physical activity is good for you. Get moving, and you can reap the benefits of higher metabolism, great muscle tone, lower body fat, and more. You can strengthen your heart and keep everything working more smoothly.

But there's a reason so many people who sign up for a gym membership in January forget they have it by February 1: going to the gym is not for everyone.

If you're one of the lucky ones who is disciplined and motivated enough to go to the gym regularly, that's great. Work with a personal trainer and design a regimen that's geared toward your goals and workout style. Whether it's bulking up or slimming down, your gym will have equipment to help you.

If you're not so inclined, however, fear not. There are other ways to get your body moving that don't require a gym membership. Here are some ideas to get you started:

- If you like the equipment you find in a gym but don't have the motivation to drag yourself to the building itself, look into purchasing a piece or two of workout equipment, free weights, etc. to have in your home. Be sure to look for pieces geared toward your fitness goals (i.e. treadmill for cardio, weights for strength training, etc.). If cost is a concern, check out Facebook marketplace or your local Buy Nothing group for possible low- or no-cost options.

- If you walk into a gym and just aren't sure what to do, look into workout classes or videos that offer a fitness regimen in line with your goals. The guidance and itinerary can help keep you on track with better results than floundering on your own. While many trainers offer apps and memberships to push you toward your goals, you can also find an abundance of videos on YouTube that cover a variety of fitness goals.

- If the idea of lifting weights or walking on a treadmill for hours at a time completely bores you, look into more engaging options. Try Zumba or dance workouts. Trust me, you'll still sweat! Or join a community sports team to get you moving and build camaraderie. The game will keep your mind off the exercise and help make it fun.

- If money is an issue, check out nature for some free and low-cost ideas: walking, hiking, bike riding, roller blading. You can also head to the local park for basketball, tennis, or swimming. Or check out videos on YouTube or DVDs from the library for no-equipment-necessary workouts.

- If you find it hard to stay motivated, try linking up with a workout buddy or group of friends. That way, when you're tempted to skip a session, you'll be disappointing others. The thought alone may keep you going, or your buddies can push you to participate. As suggested above, you can also play sports with community organizations or with a group of friends, letting you socialize and get your exercise in at the same time.

- If time is an issue, look to fit in short bursts of exercise instead of longer sessions. Walk on your lunch break or get in a quick dance workout when you first wake up.

You can also find ways to sneak in exercise without even noticing. When running errands, opt to park farther away and walk. When talking on the phone, do some stretching, squats, or toe lifts. Take the stairs instead of the elevator. Make more trips when unloading groceries from your car.

It doesn't take a full-blown workout to make an impact. Little efforts can add up. And, over time, you can increase those little efforts to more involved techniques or longer sessions. Just keep in mind that if something doesn't work with your lifestyle, it won't work — period. For me, dance workouts on the Wii and fat-burning videos on YouTube are most appealing, and I can do them with no special equipment in my spare time. Find an exercise method that will fit into your routines and personality. That is your best shot for success.

Chapter 4

Mental Health

Your mind is an amazing thing. And it has a great impact on your overall health and well-being. Just like with your body, getting your mind checked out periodically and addressing struggles you're facing can be an important part of staying healthy.

If you have concerns with your mental health, you should discuss them with a medical professional. While some things, such as mild mood swings and stress, are common, even normal, if they're affecting your life, there may be something wrong. A professional can help you with treatments and learning how to deal with ongoing issues. And getting them checked out can ensure you're living your best life.

If your concerns are within the guidelines of being "normal," you may need to find coping strategies to relieve the pressures of stress, depression, and other common mental ailments. Maintaining a balanced life, with time for both relaxation and self care in addition to making progress on your goals, can help keep your mind at ease. If you find yourself struggling, however, try the suggestions below.

Stress

Few, if any, of us can say that we live stress-free. It's part of life, and it does have a purpose. The results of stress can help us deal with moments of crisis and stir us to action. But too much stress can negatively impact our health, encouraging problems from heart issues to gastrointestinal concerns. So how do we take control of our health and cut back on our stress levels? It can be easier said than done. Fortunately, however, there are some ideas that may help you.

The first step is to figure out what's causing you the stress. If a particular situation, person, or item on your to-do list is creating your stress, identifying it and dealing with it can be the most effective solution. This means you're taking care of the cause, not just the symptoms. Get that to-do list item checked off; avoid that person as much as possible or clear the air and discuss your concerns with them; figure out what about that situation is bothering you and see if you can resolve it. If the cause cannot be taken care of, however, there are ways to deal with the symptoms that may bring you relief.

- Get pampered — Massage is a popular choice, as is any method of pampering: manicures and pedicures, salon and spa treatments such as facials, relaxing in a hot tub. These can help loosen your muscles and get you to breathe easier, leaving your mind free to deal with the stressful situation.

- Move — Physical activity can also let your mind clear. Take a walk, go for a hike, or ride a bike. Go to the gym. Play a sport with friends. Dance. Sing. Do yoga. Then, after you've exerted yourself, take a warm shower or bath to soothe your muscles and let your body unwind.

- Meditate — Try simply taking deep breaths. Sit in a comfortable chair with your hands on your lap. Close your eyes and take deep breaths, inhaling through your nose and exhaling through your mouth. Focus only on your breathing. Let your shoulders sag, your muscles relax. Roll your neck. The longer you're able to focus on your breathing, the better. Let the stress melt off you.

- Distract yourself — Sometimes the best cure for stress is getting your mind off it. Participate in an activity that brings you joy. Do you have a hobby you enjoy? Are there friends you like to socialize with? Is there a food or activity that gets your mind off everything else? Go out to the movies. Read a book. Listen to music.

* Help others — To really get your mind off your own problems, try helping others who are less fortunate. Doing volunteer work can make your situation seem a whole lot simpler. Check out https://www.volunteermatch.org/for ideas and opportunities or call your local social services department to find out where you can help.

* Take action — I find that if I'm stressed about a situation, taking actions to improve that situation brings me the greatest relief. Then I feel like I'm actually doing something instead of avoiding it. Even if the solution has not been found, and the cause is not completely dealt with, at least I know I'm getting there. And that can help relieve stress in the long-term, not just the present.

Depression

Another common ailment is depression. By this, I am referring to temporary depression caused by situations that bring sadness, worry, and discouragement.

Note: If you suffer from depression that does not go away, please consult a medical professional. You may have a chemical imbalance or other underlying problem that needs to be addressed.

I find that the most common reason I fall into a state of depression is feeling helpless. I feel like everything is spinning out of control, and that there isn't a way for me to get what I want. Life happens, and my plans keep getting put on the back burner.

When that happens, the best solution I've come up with is evaluating the situation and making a game plan to dig myself out. As much as everything seems out of your control, there has to be *something* you can control. Grab onto that and take charge, even if it has nothing to do with your long-term goals. Control what you can control, and the rest will follow:

- House a mess? Take some time to clean it. An organized home can put you in a much better state of mind. I've often heard that a cluttered home leads to a cluttered mind, leaving you less room and freedom to think about and do the things you really want to do. And I can definitely attest to that! Even if you can't clean everything, cleaning even one small space can help you feel better.

- Kids complaining? Spend some time with them. Knowing you spent quality time with them can make it easier when you need a little time away — for both you and them.

- Bogged down at work? Assess your situation, take care of as many things as you can quickly and put forth a game plan to take care of the rest. When work isn't occupying your mind, you can focus on other things.

Once you've taken control of *something*, you'll likely start to feel better about life as a whole.

When all else fails, take some time for yourself, get in touch with something you like to do, and relieve some of your stress. If you don't know what will help, here are some ideas to get you started:

Take your mind off your grumpiness:

- Participate in a hobby or pastime that makes you happy

- Read a book

- Watch a TV show or movie

- Treat yourself to a favorite food

- Make a list of what you're thankful for

Get your blood pumping

- Take a walk

- Go for a hike

- Ride a bicycle

- Play a sport with friends

- Dance or sing

Take deep breaths

- Meditate

- Take a bubble bath

- Listen to relaxing music

- Light some aromatherapy candles

Do a good deed

- Volunteer

- Perform a random act of kindness for a neighbor or acquaintance

- Donate something

Spend time with loved ones

- Go to a fair or festival

- Go shopping

- Have a picnic

- Play a board game or card game together

Whatever you decide to do, have a good time. Taking a break from reality can be the best thing to relieve stress and depression — not only help your mood but actually boost productivity in the long run.

Chapter 5

MAINTENANCE

While working to get your body in good working order is great, maintaining that level of care is just as important. Get regular physicals and check-ups with your medical providers. Not only will they let you know how you're doing — and catch potential problems early — they'll also give you an opportunity to talk to your doctor about any concerns that have arisen. You can ask questions, get checked out, and see what you need to do to keep yourself in good shape.

Getting Better

If you have medical concerns, discuss them with your medical practitioner. Make sure you're keeping up with any recommendations, such as vitamins and medications, diet, and fitness regimens. Knowing what you should do to put yourself in the best position possible can help put you in control and make you feel like you can change your life. Even if you can't control everything, controlling the controllables can help you both physically and mentally.

Monitoring Your Progress

Keeping track of how you're advancing in your health goals can not only keep you motivated to keep going but can also ensure the actions you're taking are having the desired effects.

If your goal is to lose weight, monitoring your progress is easy: just weigh yourself. But if you're working out while you're losing weight, the simple number can be deceiving. As a result, you may want to calculate your body fat and measurements as well. That way you know if you're losing fat weight even as you're gaining muscle weight.

To monitor eating or workout habits, try keeping a journal. Keep track of what you eat, when you work out, and even what actions encourage what you eat or when you work out (i.e. eating junk food when you're stressed, working out when you're angry, etc.). Knowing what you do and why you do it can help guide you in your actions and help you modify your thinking and doing so you're successful in your ultimate goal.

To monitor your progress when it comes to medical concerns, such as blood pressure, cholesterol, and certain diseases and disorders, you will likely need to partner with your doctor. He or she can order tests and help you stack on track with medications, dietary restrictions, and other guidelines. Your doctor can also give you guidance in what your ultimate goal should be and how to not only reach it but keep yourself there.

Alternative Medicine

If you're not a fan of modern medical establishments, there are alternative medical practices that can help you as well: chiropractic, acupuncture, nutrition response testing, and others. Whether you have an aversion to doctors or just prefer a more natural method of treatment, these alternative options can help you succeed in your goals. Just be advised that there are limits, and alternative medicine may not be able to address all of your concerns.

- Massage therapy — Known mainly for relieving stress, massage can also stimulate and soothe muscles and increase range of motion.

- Hypnotherapy — By placing you in a hypnotic trance, the hypnotist taps into your subconscious to locate underlying concerns and help you move past grievances or addictions.

- Acupuncture — Various spots on your body act as pressure points. Stimulating these spots can have a reaction on different parts of your body. By inserting ultra-thin needles at precise locations on your body, an acupuncturist can use these pressure points to heal, specifically in cases of pain or nausea.

- Chiropractic — By applying pressure and "cracking" certain areas of the spine, the chiropractor will realign the spine. This can relieve pain and pressure along the spine and relieve symptoms throughout the body.

- Nutrition Response Testing — Using the same pressure points as acupuncture, the practitioner will locate weak points in your body. He or she does this by applying pressure on the pressure point and pushing on your raised arm to detect strength or weakness. In the case of weakness, supplements are placed on your body and the process is repeated to determine which supplements will help your concerns. As time passes, supplements may be added or subtracted, and dietary changes may be made to fine-tune issues and rid your body of toxins and weakness.

To learn more about these alternative medicines, or to find someone who practices them, search online or ask others for recommendations. As alternative methods have gained popularity, you may find that many people you know have utilized these techniques or others.

As with anything that alters or affects your body, each of these methods may have risks in addition to the perceived benefits. Be sure to get all of the information you can before partaking.

Chapter 6

Extra Help

No matter what your health goals are, other people are likely going through the same thing. Whether it's losing weight, starting an exercise program, eating better, or dealing with a particular disease or ailment, you are not alone. As a result, you will find a variety of websites to help you in your journey. In Chapter 1 of this section, I listed sites to help you find a doctor, optometrist, and dentist. If you don't have a doctor yet, I encourage you to start with that, before tackling any specific goals or self-diagnosing.

General Information

For overall medical information, my favorite site is WebMd (https://www.webmd.com/). I can search by symptoms, or get general information, home treatments, and tips on when to call my doctor. While it's not a replacement for actually seeing a doctor, it can be a helpful tool when you have a quick question or want to find out what that symptom might mean, especially when your doctor's office might be closed.

The Mayo Clinic (https://www.mayoclinic.org/) is another valuable source of helpful information and research tools that can help you.

When I was pregnant and was a new mother, I found The Bump (https://www.thebump.com/) helpful. Not only do they have articles in which they answer questions, but they also have a variety of forums on the site to help anyone who is trying to conceive, who is pregnant, or who has a child. Discussing ideas and concerns with others can help you feel connected and give you peace of mind.

These sites, however, are certainly not the only ones out there.

Specific Diseases

If you're looking for information on a particular disease or ailment, your best bet would be to do an internet search or ask your medical provider for recommendations. There are simply too many categories to list here! Visit your favorite search engine and type in the disease or ailment you're looking for information on. If you're trying to find a support group or forum, search for "forum: disease or ailment," replacing "disease or ailment" with the actual disease or ailment you're looking for. You'll find plenty of books, websites, and forums that can help you get information and guidance.

Losing Weight, Getting Healthy

When it comes to losing weight, starting a fitness regime, or eating healthier, the material out there tends to overlap. Therefore the sites below cover multiple categories. And some sites will also offer forums, making them a valuable resource to discuss your goals and progress with others.

- LosingWeight: https://losingweight.com/

- Livestrong: https://www.livestrong.com/

- Healthline: https://www.healthline.com/

Keep in mind that some weight loss programs, such as Weight Watchers and Jenny Craig, also offer online components to their programs, whcih can be valuable tools as well if you find yourself needing extra help in those goals.

Other Resources

Websites are not the only tools out there to help you succeed in your goals. Search for health apps on your smart device to find everything from calorie counters to pedometers to personal trainers, yoga, healthy recipes, relaxing sounds, and more. You can even find apps to help you quick smoking, train for a marathon, or learn emergency first aid.

Books and magazines can also be valuable tools that offer not only information but quick references on a variety of topics. Check out your local library to browse and find the right choices for you.

Part Five

Relationships

Chapter 1

GETTING STARTED

Our lives are often defined by our relationships with others, whether they're romantic relationships, familial relationships, or working relationships. We are a social species, and we are drawn to other human beings. But that doesn't mean our relationships are perfect. Often they need a little help to get them to a place we're comfortable with.

Start with Yourself

Relationships can encounter many different types of problems, from communication issues and differences of opinion to infidelity or even abuse. When it comes to taking charge of your relationships, there are many things to consider, and we'll tackle them in the coming chapters. But the first step to handling any kind of relationship is looking at your role in it. It takes more than one person to be in a relationship, and to make any changes, you have to acknowledge and accept your part. I'm not blaming you for any issues in your relationships. I'm simply reminding you that you can't control someone else's actions. You can only control your reactions to them.

Maybe you'll ultimately decide a relationship isn't worth saving, or you'll admit defeat when the other person involved doesn't want to make the effort. Or maybe you'll decide on a whole different course of action to find contentment. Regardless of the ultimate outcome, the changes you make to yourself and your role in your relationships will help you in the future. You'll be stronger, more confident, and more capable of dealing with whatever comes your way. So look within.

Okay, easy to say. But what does that mean?

1. The first step is to stop assigning blame. Even if the initial break or current problem in a relationship was started by someone else, your reaction played just as much of a role in what resulted. And if you've decided the relationship is worth salvaging, you need to adjust your reaction. Instead of just blaming the other person, think about what role you may have played.

2. Make the first move. Don't expect someone else to act first. Be the bigger person and take that step. If may mean swallowing a little bit of pride, but it will also give you some control.

3. Acknowledge your role — not only to yourself, but to the other person or people. Again, swallow your pride and accept some of the responsibility. Even if you've already admitted to yourself you were part of it, saying it out loud will demonstrate that you're serious about repairing whatever damage has occurred. And it may make the other(s) involved more receptive to taking the next steps.

4. Start a dialogue. Open the lines of communication so you can really get somewhere in mending your relationship.

Ideally the person you're communicating with will also acknowledge his or her role, and the relationship will be back on firmer footing. But let's face it, that doesn't always happen. The other people may not be willing to acknowledge their role in the problem. You need to decide if that's a dealbreaker or something you're willing to work with. Anything worth having is worth fighting for, but only you can decide if that relationship is worth having.

Lack of a Relationship

Ever hear the phrase "you can't love someone else until you love yourself"? Yes, it's hard finding Mr. or Miss Right. It can be hard to find devoted friends. It can be hard to have meaningful relationships with your family members. But before you can even be in a quality relationship, you need to be ready. Are you happy with yourself? Do you like yourself? Do you consider yourself a worthwhile human being?

If your answer to any of those questions was "no," you need to first take control of your most important relationship — your relationship with yourself.

If you truly have difficulty accepting your worth, there are many books, podcasts, and other resources available to help you. You can also seek professional help in the form of a psychologist or therapist. Take some time to work on building your self-esteem and appreciating yourself. Believe that you are a worthwhile human being. You have a unique personality and skills that are truly yours. No one else can be you. Rather than shy away from your unique traits, embrace them. Be you!

Here are some ideas to get you started:

- Make a list of what you love about yourself

- Make a list of areas in which you excel

- Determine your favorites: part of your body, personality quirk, thing that makes you unique

- Think about why you're not happy with yourself — then find reasons they're all lies

If there really is something you have a problem with, do something about it. This whole book is about creating the life you want, and that includes being the person you want to be. Whether you feel you're a bit overweight or not educated enough or too shy, you can take steps that will make you happier in the skin you're in.

It may feel awkward in the beginning, but once you're comfortable with yourself, then you can look outward. As your confidence builds, you can work on making the first move, putting yourself out there, and being yourself on those ever-important dates or social events. After all, being you is pretty great.

While you're working on yourself, be sure you don't go a bit *too* far. Just as a lack of confidence can discourage potential mates and companions, so can an egotistical streak. Relationships are a two-way street, so make sure you balance you with the person you're with. Don't just talk about yourself. And don't disregard his or her feelings. Reflect your personality and let your companion reflect his or her personality, as well.

Now that we've got that covered, let's jump in!

Chapter 2

ROMANCE

Whether it's starting a relationship, altering a current one, or deciding to end one, making the decision to change your current romantic situation can affect many aspects of your life. But if you're unhappy with the current status of your love life, changing it will likely have a positive impact on your life.

Starting a Relationship

Let's face it, some things are out of your control. You can't make Mr. or Miss Right walk down the street and bump into you. And you can't make someone fall in love with you. But you can put yourself out there and make yourself available for the right person to find you. As discussed in the previous chapter, however, before you can be ready for someone else, you need to be ready for yourself. Being happy with who you are is the first step toward being in a worthwhile relationship. Know who you are, be comfortable with your self-worth, and know that you deserve to be in the relationship you want. An added bonus? Confidence is sexy and will make you more appealing when the right person does come along.

That being said, when you're ready to find your second half, continue being true to yourself. If you're not one for bar-hopping or clubbing, don't start hitting the town to try and find your match. The people you meet won't be in line with what you're looking for. At the same time, if you're a social butterfly, don't look for your mate in the science fiction section of the closest Barnes & Noble. Think about the kind of person you are, the kind of person you want to meet, and the qualities you hope to share. The possibilities are endless when it comes to places to meet your soul mate, and knowing what you're looking for should steer you in the right direction.

When I was ready to be in a relationship, I realized that I didn't have a lot of opportunities to meet men. I wasn't into the night club scene. I didn't drink. And I was self-employed, so I didn't even have coworkers who could fix me up. I was a bit of a homebody, so even my friends were few (by choice). I was in a pickle. I decided to go online. That was many years ago now, and while it's become more popular, I was still a bit nervous. But online I was able to be picky about who I was and what I was looking for. I communicated with a few people before I met my husband. Some of the people I talked to were a little strange; some just weren't a good fit. It actually didn't take long to connect with my husband, and, while I can't say it was love at first sight, we meshed well, and the rest is history. But I never would have met him if I didn't put myself out there or if I had looked in all the wrong places.

If you're ready to put yourself out there and meet people, I've come up with a list of suggestions on where to look to get started.

Online

Online dating sites are definitely popular. And the possibilities continue to grow. You'll find free services and paid services, platforms that cater to clientele with certain criteria in common, such as religious affiliation or ethnic group, and sites that focus more on physical relationships than lasting connection. With the ever-changing offerings, listing them here would be impractical. Your best bet is to search online or through your app store and find platforms that appeal to you. It may require some trial and error and investigation, but finding a good fit can be almost as important as finding the right partner.

Another online option, if dating sites are not your thing, is to connect with people in online forums and social media groups. You can meet others with similar interests in a casual atmosphere. Just keep in mind that you may end up with more friends than romantic possibilities.

Public Places

They say a great place to meet people is at the grocery store. I can't attest to this, but enough people have said it that there must be some truth to it! Grocery stores aside, however, you can also meet people at other establishments, such as bookstores or coffee shops. Starting a conversation with a stranger can require a bit of confidence and an extroverted nature, but you never know who you might run into and connect with.

You can also try the cliched bar scene, where you can find many singles looking to connect. Depending on the atmosphere of the bar you choose, you may find young singles just looking to "hook up" or you may find more mature singles looking for a real relationship. Ask friends and coworkers for suggestions or do your homework before popping up in a bar that's not what you're looking for.

Beyond the bar, you can also try other public spaces, such as parks, the gym, the library, and more. Maintain a friendly, open personality, and you'll open yourself up to the opportunities as they present themselves.

Other Options

Though often ridiculed by the books and movies criticizing blind dates and the like, meeting someone by way of introduction is a well-established option. Let close friends and family know you are looking for someone. If they know you well, they may find you the perfect match. You can also try putting yourself out there in a group setting, such as with a class, team, club, or religious group. If that part of your life is important to you, having that connection can be a great starting point. Try volunteering and joining new groups to meet more people. If you're feeling a little more adventurous, you can also check out options like speed-dating, in which you meet several potential partners and interact for only a short time to see if you're compatible.

Keeping a Relationship

Keep in mind that meeting that special someone isn't the end. To form a lasting relationship, you have to be yourself and accept him or herself for who he or she is, too. Pretending to be someone you're not, or expecting the person you're with to be someone he or she is not, will only set you up for disappointment. Even if it got all the way to "I do," it's unlikely you'd be able to continue the charade for the rest of your life. And would you really want to?

Making Changes

Not everyone needs help finding someone or forming a lasting relationship. But that doesn't mean everything is wonderful. Maybe your relationship isn't satisfying you. Maybe something needs to change. Or maybe it needs to end.

Ideally, any relationship you're in will meet your expectations, make you feel safe and happy, and bring you fulfillment. In reality, it's not that simple. As humans, we're all different, and it's natural that we'll have different expectations and different ways of looking at things. There will be conflict. There will be tension. And even if you're happy overall with each other, there will be times you simply don't see eye-to-eye.

Maybe you have different visions of what your lives together will entail — live together or separately? marriage or no marriage? kids or no kids? buy or rent a home? east coast or west coast? focus on career or focus on family? spend or save? The possibilities for conflict are endless. And even if personalities mesh well, life goals may not.

Small day-to-day disagreements are normal. You won't always agree, and as long as you can be open and respectful, these small issues should blow over fairly quickly. If you find yourself butting heads on major issues, however, sit down with your significant other and discuss what you really want. Avoid attacking your partner. Instead, explain how certain things are important to you. Compromise is important in a relationship, and perhaps some things can be compromised on. But make sure you're not compromising on something that truly is important to you. If you've always wanted kids and your significant other does not, will you be happy never being a parent? Will you end up resenting your partner because of it? As painful as it might be to have these discussions now, it's a whole lot easier than dealing with the aftermath. Many issues can be worked out. But if they can't be, it's better to know now. Be careful when having these discussions, though. Issuing ultimatums can just build resentment, which helps no one.

If you find yourself constantly being defensive or not trusting your partner, step back and evaluate the situation. Are you giving your significant other a chance? Are you seeing him or her for who he or she really is, or are you projecting your own insecurities onto him or her? Make sure the things you're arguing about are real — not your interpretations of what's taking place. If you truly can't trust your partner, that's a problem. But if you're just looking for reasons to be upset, that's on you.

If, however, you've followed my previous recommendations, and you accept yourself for who you are, and acknowledge the person you're with for who he or she is, you should have a pretty good idea if you get along well. If you're constantly fighting, maybe you aren't meant to be together. If you seem to bring out the worst in each other, maybe you would be better apart. Likewise, if your partner is not accepting *you* for who *you* are, and is frequently belittling what is important to you, he or she is likely not right for you. Recognizing what you really want is the first step to determining how to proceed. If you're unhappy, even miserable, most of the time, it's time to part ways.

Parting Ways

When conflicts become too much to bear, or you simply realize that this relationship is not the right one for you, it's time to have the dreaded talk.

With any luck the person you've been seeing feels the same way. If not, prepare for some defensiveness and backlash.

Just remember: there is a reason you're at this point. It doesn't help anyone to be in a relationship that makes you miserable. Dragging things out does just that — drag them out. It doesn't make them better. It just makes them last longer. Be firm but gentle. You don't need to attack or berate the person you're breaking up with. Be civil and hopefully the experience will be as pain-free as possible.

Important Note

If you are in an abusive relationship and need help getting out of it, please seek help. I am not an expert in this area and would not want to give you harmful advice, but many organizations exist specifically for that purpose. Just remember that you are a worthwhile human being, and no one deserves to be in a relationship that hurts them mentally, emotionally, or physically. You deserve better.

Chapter 3

FAMILY

"Family" can encompass a lot of people: parents, siblings, grandparents, aunts, uncles, cousins, spouses, children, even pets. Your relationships with some or all of them may be strained, whether it's a personality conflict or they did something that really bothered you. Or maybe you're looking to enhance your relationships, get closer to some of your family members. Maybe you want to add to your family by having a child or adopting a pet. Regardless of how you want your family relationships to change, here is some guidance.

Your Relatives

They're the people in your life you didn't pick: your blood relations who may or may not bring you joy. If you're content in your relationships with them, you likely don't need this section. But if they drive you crazy (and not in a good way!) and you find yourself avoiding them, perhaps it's time to evaluate your relationships and see what to do about them.

If you want to have a close relationship with family members who have certain qualities or past actions that have hurt you, it may be time to sit down and talk to them. As with romantic relationships, communication can be key to having a healthy relationship with those close to you. Don't attack the other person, but rather explain how you feel, and how what they do or did affected you. Sometimes others won't realize how their actions have affected you. Or hearing their side can make you understand why they did what they did.

If you're not satisfied with the other person's response, or that person is not apologetic for what you perceive to be wrongdoings, it's time to make a choice. If you want to have a relationship with them, then you may have to learn to let some things go. While you can never forget who they are or what they've done, you have to accept them for who they are — flaws and all — and forgive them for their actions. It's not about forgetting what they did or who they are; it's about accepting it and not letting it consume you and your relationship. Can you do that? If not, the relationship is likely not salvageable. If your interactions will constantly be tainted by memories and teeth-grinding, you may opt to instead limit your interactions as much as possible. But if you truly want to build a relationship with them, look inside yourself and think about what you can accept.

If the other person has acknowledged their role in making you unhappy, and/or you have accepted that role, then you can work on finding ways to build the relationship. Spend time together, find common ground to discuss, and look for opportunities to strengthen your bond.

Your Spouse

All relationships require work, but these are perhaps the most crucial. You love your spouse (theoretically). You have chosen to spend your life with him or her. Where you live, what you do, how you act — chances are they're all affected by your spouse and the decision to be together.

If you're at the point of divorce, I won't try to talk you out of it. I've been in that position, and I believe you have to do what's right for you. But I will ask this: are you sure? Have you looked at your relationship and determined there's no way to fix what's wrong? Only you can answer that question, and only you can make the ultimate decision. I would just encourage you to make sure that is what you truly want.

That being said, what could use improving in your relationship? Chances are there's something. Everyone has little quirks that annoy others. It's just human nature. But if there's something that truly needs changing, sit down and talk about it. Talk about what's missing, what's not working, what needs help. Try not to get defensive or attack your spouse. This is supposed to bring you closer, not drive you further apart. Do you need more affection? Do you need help around the house? Support in a decision you've made? Feedback on a career change? No matter what it is, talk about it. Not only will it help you get what you need, but it can also bring you closer.

Be sure the conversation isn't one-sided, though. If you've been feeling some tension, chances are your partner has, as well. Listen to what he or she says, what he or she needs. And don't brush off his or her concerns. Listen and respond accordingly. For your relationship to work, you need to be able to give as well as take. And don't forget to thank your spouse for actions he or she has taken that address your needs. Everyone wants to feel appreciated.

While you are discussing your concerns, or any time arguments arise, make sure you are not only listening to your partner but looking for ways to work together, find compromise, and resolve differences. Consider each other's needs when working to solve problems.

If you and your spouse are having difficulty communicating or finding common ground, consider bringing in a marriage counselor. Having an objective third party involved can keep you on track and ensure that disagreements don't escalate into screaming matches. They can also offer suggestions and guidance to bring the two of you closer.

Kids

When it comes to kids, your concerns can cover a variety of topics: starting a family, bonding, behavioral issues, development concerns, etc. We will discuss starting a family in a moment, but first, let's tackle other possible issues.

To start, take a good look at your kids. They may be driving you crazy, but that's nothing to be concerned about. You need to determine if there are underlying issues that are creating challenges or causing your relationship with your child to be strained. Each child will have his or her own personality. That is what makes them unique. Are you accepting them for who they are, or are you trying to project onto them who you want them to be? While you may not always like some of their personality quirks, trying to change them into people they're not can not only cause your child to act out and rebel; it can also cause irreparable damage in the form of strained relationships or repercussions from actions taken while acting out. If damage has already been done, take a similar course of action as you would with other family members. Open lines of communication and see what can be repaired.

If you suspect your child has underlying concerns, such as medical issues or behavioral troubles, seek help. Books, doctors, counselors, and support groups can all help you understand your child and learn how to help him or her. If you're not sure if there's anything to worry about, getting professional help can let you know that, too.

Above all, though, try to accept your children for who they are. Spend time with them, listen to them, embrace their uniqueness. Take part in their interests. Show them you love them. Make sure they feel wanted, loved, and accepted. That is when the bonding really happens.

Starting a Family

If having children is your concern, then, obviously, your course of action is quite different. Starting a family is a big decision, and even if you're mentally, emotionally, and financially prepared, the path is not always easy. Medical issues, in particular, can be a big barrier in having a child. When my husband and I decided we wanted to start a family, we had trouble conceiving, and for us, there ended up being an underlying medical concern that needed to be addressed.

Deciding to take charge of your life can't make medical issues go away. But it can give you the determination to figure out what can be done about them, and what can be done if they can't be resolved. Start by getting all of the information you can. When we were having trouble, we talked with healthcare providers to determine what was going on. And we discussed our options. If we hadn't been able to conceive, we considered adoption. Not conceiving naturally doesn't mean you have to give up on your dream of becoming a parent. Modern medicine combined with societal structures mean you have more options than ever, from sperm donation to surrogacy, IVF to steroid injections, fostering to adoption. Many of these options also apply if your barrier to parenthood is not being in a relationship, or being in a same-sex relationship that means natural conception isn't an option. Evaluate all of your options and determine the best course of action for your family.

If you're having difficulty conceiving, or you want to open your heart and home to one of the thousands of children looking for a family, adoption is certainly a worthwhile option.

Adoption, as with any decision to add to your family, is not to be taken lightly. If the child is older, he or she may have special needs or emotional scarring from previous experiences. And regardless of the age of the child, he or she needs love, support, and care — for life. Taking a child into your family means being there for him or her and providing for that child physically and emotionally. Adoption can also be expensive, and the wait time for a child can be lengthy, especially if you're looking for a newborn.

If this is something you are considering, do your research. The adoption process is lengthy and complicated. Do an internet search for "adoption resources," and you'll be bombarded with websites full of information and support. Before getting overwhelmed, start by asking yourself some questions:

- Am I capable of raising a child?

- Do I have the necessary income to support a child? Can I afford the adoption process fees?

- What age child am I looking for? Race? Nationality?

- Do I want to adopt from my own country or abroad?

- Am I willing to adopt a child with special needs?

- Am I willing to adopt siblings or do I just want a single child?

- Do I want to be a foster parent with the intent to adopt, or do I only want to adopt directly?

And these are just the beginning. To really get started, check out https://adoption.com/ for more information and guidance in the adoption process. While it can be lengthy, if you're willing to take on the time and expense involved, you can be matched with a child to love and welcome into your family.

Pets

Animals can be a welcome addition to any family. They offer love and affection and even medical benefits. From what I've read, they can help diminish the chance of allergies in children, reduce stress, and help the elderly find purpose and an improved quality of life.

Just like kids, pets need love, attention, medical care, and basic needs taken care of. If you want to welcome an animal into your home, make sure you're able and willing to meet all these needs before taking a life into your hands.

Plenty of pet stores sell pets, or you can opt to adopt a pet instead of purchase one, to help an animal in need. We had a dog who was a rescue, found in a vacated apartment, locked inside a bathroom with nothing to eat or drink. He was abandoned, starved, and desperately in need of a loving home. We found him through https://www.petfinder.com/, but that's certainly not the only way to locate a pet in need. Check out your local animal shelter or humane society. Browse your local newspaper or online listings for pets in need of homes. Even radio and television stations will at times host events for pet adoptions.

Pet adoptions still have costs, which usually go toward the initial care of the animal before you took over. The animal was likely treated by a vet, perhaps spayed or neutered, and vaccinated, plus there were boarding and feeding costs. Be prepared to dish out a few hundred dollars to cover these expenses, plus the cost of any supplies you'll need.

Once you decide to bring an animal into your family, there are a few things to keep in mind:

- Our home was inspected before we were approved to adopt our dog. His foster mom visited with him to make sure the home was suitable and appropriate. Check out your home from the viewpoint of a four-legged creature to make sure everything is as it should be.

- Owning a pet has a slew of costs, including food, vet bills, medications, and supplies. Be prepared to support that animal for as long as he or she may live.

- In addition to material goods, most animals need love. Can you give a new pet the attention it needs?

- Understand that just as with human children, our furry friends can have problems. They can have health concerns, behavioral issues, and psychological scars — especially if they're rescues. Make sure you can be patient and understanding enough to take on these issues.

- And last but not least, understand that your new pet will come complete with his or her own personality. Be prepared to surrender your heart when you look into those little eyes.

Chapter 4

FRIENDS

For many of you, friends are an integral part of your life, and you wouldn't have it any other way. Then there are those who want a few confidantes or a cluster of friends and are having trouble finding them. Perhaps you just moved to a new area or you've been too busy to really nurture any friendships. Or maybe you're just really shy. No matter the reason, you can still meet new people and form lasting relationships.

Make New Friends

Meeting new friends can be much like meeting a new potential life partner. You want to find someone you "click" with, someone who shares common interests while also being different enough to keep things interesting. So where do you look? As with everything else, possibilities abound. You can check out the night scene. You can sign up for classes you're interested in. You can go online and join forums and chat groups in topics that appeal to you. Talk to your neighbors. Volunteer. Join local organizations. Join a religious establishment and talk to the leaders there about social events.

Once you've found places to meet people, go. It can be very scary to put yourself out there, but sitting at home by yourself, too scared to talk to anybody, will ensure you remain by yourself. If you're shy, start small. Chat with people online to build your confidence. Perhaps some of the forums and groups you chat in have local members. If you hit it off, arrange to meet for coffee. Once you're comfortable with yourself and what you have to offer, expand your social circle to meet other people, as well. Talk with others who share common interests. Participate in events that appeal to you and will give you the opportunity to meet others who share your passions. Give yourself the opportunity to connect with others who can be valuable additions to your life.

But Keep the Old

Relationships new and old need to be nurtured. It's not just about meeting someone, chatting them up for a bit, then calling when you need something. Friendships, just like romantic relationships, are about give and take. Be the kind of friend you want to have. Support your friends in their times of need. Lend an ear. Help with birthday parties, support their kids, and offer to help them in a pinch. Be a comedian when he or she is down. Make chicken soup when he or she is sick.

Of course that doesn't mean to let your friends' lives consume your own. To be a worthwhile friend, you still need to be a worthwhile person. Nurture yourself, as well, so you still have something to offer yourself, your friends, and the rest of the world. As I said, it's about give and take. Just as you would help your friend in a time of need, look to your friends when you need help. Not only will your friend appreciate being needed; it will also strengthen your bond and help you get closer.

Struggles

If you find that a "friend" is not the supportive, loving person that you need him or her to be, consider his or her role in your life. Is he or she just a friend you see or talk to occasionally, a peripheral member of your life? If so, then perhaps that's okay. Not everyone will be a close, vital member of your circle of friends. Is he or she going through a difficult time right now? That's okay, too. Cut him or her a little slack. There just may not be enough hours in the day at the moment for him or her to really be there for you. Offer support in the hope that once things get back on an even keel, you'll get your friend back. Is he or she the kind of person who will come to you only when he or she needs something, borrow money without repaying it, constantly say they're "too busy" when you need or want something? Then perhaps it's time to cut your losses and look for friendship elsewhere. A friend that is just a drain on your mental and physical resources without any benefit to your life is not really a friend, and, sadly, is simply not worth your time and effort. It may sound callous, but with billions of people in the world, why are you wasting your time with someone who makes you feel worse? Spend your time with those who appreciate you.

Chapter 5

CHOICES

All relationships, whether they be between friends, family members, coworkers, or significant others, will encounter times of conflict. It's simply human nature; two people will not be in agreement 100 percent of the time. Some issues will, of course, be bigger than others, but the root of it all lies in the same realm. As such, you will find yourself faced with opportunities — opportunities to deal with this conflict and determine how you'd like to proceed.

Forgiving

A lot of conflict is easily dealt with. Slight differences in opinion, minor disagreements — easily let go, easily forgiven and forgotten. But you will also encounter more intense conflict, made all the more heated because it's a matter of right and wrong — and of course, you're right.

At times like those, you have to decide: can the "wrongdoing" be forgiven? If not, can you move past it and keep your relationship intact?

The decision is ultimately yours. Depending on the severity of the wrongdoing, you may find it difficult to accept or forgive. You need to decide at that point if the relationship means more than the wrong.

If the relationship is otherwise strong, and means a great deal to you, attempting to move past it may be your preferred course of action. Perhaps having an honest conversation and trying to see things from the other person's point of view can help. Knowing the other person's reasoning and feelings can make it easier to forgive.

If the relationship was weak to begin with, or the severity of the wrong is very high, you need to decide if you want to put forth the effort required to salvage the relationship. With enough determination, chances are high that you can move past the conflict — as long as both parties are able to come to an agreement. But it won't be easy.

A suggestion as you determine your course of action: don't wait too long. The more time that passes, the harder it will be to put the past behind you. Time can leave a scar, and the effort required to salvage the relationship grows as time passes. A hiccup in the course of a relationship, no matter how big the hiccup, is easier to move past than a days-, weeks-, months-, or even years-long span of time that ruptures the relationship completely.

And if you can't forgive? Well, perhaps the relationship has run its course. Just make sure you're moving on for the right reasons. Don't let your pride interfere with a relationship worth saving. A bit of swallowed pride is easier to accept than the regrets that are sure to come.

And while we're on the subject of pride, don't be too proud to admit if you were actually in the wrong. If you have realized that you were the one to make a mistake, or cause the conflict, acknowledge it and apologize. Sometimes we're the ones who actually need forgiving.

Cutting Ties

Whether it's a romantic relationship or a friendship — or even a working relationship — it can be difficult to determine when it's time to cut your losses and say goodbye. Below are some general guidelines to consider if you're trying to decide. Of course there will always be exceptions, especially in a relationship that is longstanding and means a lot to you, but if you've gotten to the point where you're considering cutting ties, these guidelines can help.

- It's just too much work — All relationships require work. But if it seems as if you spend all your time trying to salvage the relationship, you have to ask yourself: what is it that you're trying to salvage? Is there still enough there that's worth holding onto, or are you just fighting for it because that's what you're used to doing? Relationships should be some work — but a lot of good times, too.

- All give and no take — Relationships are partnerships, regardless of who you're in a relationship with. They are about give and take, with each partner holding up his or her end of both. If you're constantly giving everything to the other person — time, love, energy, money, support, etc. — and aren't getting anything in return, that's not a partnership; it's a parasitic relationship. Though there will be times, such as during crises or emergencies, that the relationship becomes more one-sided, overall relationships should be mutually beneficial. If you reach out to help someone in their time of need, that person should be willing to return the favor when you're in need.

- You're just not happy — If on the surface everything seems to be perfect, but underneath you're miserable, that's not good, either. Relationships are about more than what's on the surface. They should bring you some kind of fulfillment — whatever that kind of relationship is meant to fill. A relationship should add value to your life and bring you happiness. If it's not doing that, you need to ask yourself why.

- Abuse — Not all kinds of abuse are easily identifiable, though if you're in a relationship that is obviously mentally or physically abusive — get out! You deserve better. If you're not sure, think about how you feel when you're with the other person. Are you afraid? Do you flinch when he or she approaches? Do you hesitate from doing things because you're concerned how the other will react? Have you distanced yourself from family or friends? Even if the "good" times make you happy, if the "bad" times outweigh them — especially if you answered "yes" to any of the questions I just asked — you should seriously consider getting out of the relationship. Seek professional help if you need it. There are many resources available to people in abusive relationships, and you shouldn't have to live in fear. Your life is precious, and you deserve to be happy. Call 211 or visit the National Domestic Violence Hotline at https://www.thehotl ine.org/.

Chapter 6

MAINTENANCE

Relationships aren't easy. They're about more than just hanging out with someone here and there. They require maintenance to keep them healthy and strong.

Communication

Every relationship we have uses communication to flourish, whether that communication is verbal or nonverbal. We communicate our wants and needs. We express our emotions. We show how we care for those who are important to us.

A lack of communication can tear down relationships in an instant. That's why it's important to keep lines of communication open. If a relationship is already severed or damaged, reopening those lines can be the key to repairing the damage.

Evaluate your relationships, particularly those that you want to change or repair. How are your lines of communication? Are you able to speak freely? Is there tension? Now think about the relationships you want to have with those people. Is it possible to sit down with them and discuss your concerns, your wishes, your hopes? Are there perhaps situations that may have been misread, or misunderstandings or miscommunication that caused a break in the relationship? Would discussing those situations help heal the damage?

Once you've made the decision to open lines of communication, think about your approach. Appearing too confrontational can cause additional strain. The purpose is to express your thoughts and emotions, but attacking the person you're communicating with doesn't solve anything. Instead, think about what you want to say, pause before saying anything, and try to stay calm. If you find it hard to start a conversation or don't know what to say, think about what you can *do* to communicate your feelings instead. Can you show the person you care through your actions?

On the flip-side, holding back how you really feel can cause resentment or frustration. Just going along with whatever he or she says doesn't solve anything, either — and may cause more damage as you keep your real emotions bottled up inside, ready to explode. Take a deep breath, formulate your thoughts, and express yourself. You might be surprised at the results.

Even in relationships that aren't strained, having regular conversations to discuss wants, needs, and thoughts can help keep those relationships healthy. It can also help move your relationship forward. For example, when I was anxious to start a family, I talked about it with my husband to see how he was feeling. I wanted to make sure he was ready to try, too. We discussed fears, concerns, desires, and ultimately decided to start trying. But if we hadn't had that conversation (those conversations, actually), we never would have gotten to that point. We needed to communicate to know we were on the same page, that we wanted the same things. Even in less important matters, this is critical. Without communication, we would never know how the other person was thinking, feeling, or reading a situation. And that information is key to keeping your relationships healthy.

Quality Time

Whether it's spent snuggling on the couch with your significant other or having a heart-to-heart chat with your best friend, your relationships also need time to thrive. Any relationship, whether it's between parents and children, partners, friends, etc., needs quality time to strength bonds and create a connection. It doesn't have to be a lot of time, as long as you make the effort and give it the attention it deserves. Focus on and enjoy the time together.

It all comes down to a feeling. Do you feel connected with those you care about, or do you feel like you're drifting apart? If it's the latter, perhaps you need to find more time to strengthen the relationship. Do something fun together or just spend time in each other's company. It will take effort to maintain a connection, but it's worth it. Do what you can so your loved ones don't slip away.

Chapter 7

Extra Help

When you think of "online" and "relationships," you probably think about online dating sites. But the internet has many relationship resources beyond dating sites, from advice to quizzes to forums, for all kinds of relationships, not just romantic. If you're looking for help, there are plenty of places to find it.

General Information

When it comes to general relationship advice, tips, and ideas, articles abound. Below are some sites dedicated to relationships that can help guide you in your life:

- LifeTips (general): https://relationship.lifetips.com/

- Oprah (general): https://www.oprah.com/app/relationships.html

- WebMD (romantic): https://www.webmd.com/sex-relationships/default.htm

- Psychology Today (romantic): https://www.psychologytoday

.com/us/basics/relationships

Articles can inform you of the latest studies, offer suggestions and guidance, and encourage you in your quest to improve your relationships. There's certainly no shortage of information! But keep in mind that every relationship is different, and that articles and advice are not the be-all and end-all when it comes to determining your course of action. What they can do, however, is offer valuable information that can help if you're stuck or need some motivation.

Forums

Sometimes it can help to have objective people offer their insight on your current situation. This can help you get ideas or look at things from a different point of view. It can also help to weigh in on others' situations; you can help others and possibly gain new perspective on your own relationships. Below are some places that can help get you started with connecting with others online:

- Talk About Marriage: https://www.talkaboutmarriage.com/

- eNotAlone: https://www.enotalone.com/

- LoveShack.org: https://www.loveshack.org/

You can also find forums by going to your favorite search engine and searching for "forum: topic" (just replace "topic" with the actual topic you want to discuss).

Other Resources

In addition to online resources, you can also find valuable information in books and magazines on many relationship topics. Search for reputable, qualified sources that can offer you real advice.

And don't forget that the most valuable resources are the people you're in relationships with. Talk to them, spend time with them, share your hopes and fears. Many problems can be resolved by simply opening our hearts and minds to the people around us.

Part Six

MAKING A DIFFERENCE

Chapter 1

GETTING STARTED

The internet and other media have truly made our world a global community. While that's great as far as education and communication are concerned, it can also increase awareness of all the people and causes who could use our help. If you're feeling the urge to truly make a difference in the lives of others, then this section of the book is for you.

There are many ways to make a difference, from writing a check to traveling across the globe to help out firsthand. Regardless of what works for you, help is appreciated and gives not only those you help but you yourself a sense of fulfillment and wellbeing.

Contributing usually falls into a few main categories, though the subcategories and specifics can vary widely:

Donating

The quickest, simplest way to contribute is by writing a check (or the monetary or electronic equivalent!). Money can go a long way toward helping people and organizations who need help. Just make sure you're familiar with the organizations you're contributing to. Not all groups are reputable, and even some reputable organizations may be questionable when it comes to the percentage of monetary donations that are applied to actually doing good. Check out Charity Navigator (https://www.charitynavigator.org/) or Charity Watch (https://www.charitywatch.org/) to research organizations you're interested in helping.

In addition to monetary donations, you can also donate items that are needed: food, clothing, toiletries, and more. Look for groups advertising food and clothing drives or inquire at your town's social services department to find out how to donate. Items often go directly to those who need them, ensuring your donation is truly being put to good use. Other places to donate, such as Goodwill and Salvation Army stores, will sell the items you donate and use the proceeds to fund their efforts. Decide which format appeals most to you.

Volunteering

When it comes to local groups and organizations, volunteering is a great way to help out, especially if you don't have the monetary resources to donate or simply want a more hands-on way to give back. And if you have a specific skill or talent, there's probably a group who would love to utilize it. If you're particularly ambitious, you can even join an organization that will send you around the country or even the world to help others with disaster relief and ongoing needs.

To find volunteer opportunities, check out VolunteerMatch (https://www.volunteermatch.org/) or AmeriCorps (https://americorps.gov/serve). Or reach out to local groups and organizations in your area to find out if they could use a helping hand. Don't forget places like nursing homes and hospitals that offer worthwhile opportunities to truly connect with other people.

Mentoring

If working with children is your forte, and you're interested in helping at-risk kids, consider mentoring. You can coach, tutor, or just be a friend willing to lend a hand and a sympathetic ear. Check out Mentoring.or g (https://www.mentoring.org/take-action/become-a-mentor/) to look for opportunities. You can also inquire at your town's social services department about local opportunities or reach out to organizations such as Big Brothers Big Sisters of America (https://www.bbbs.org/get-invo lved/become-a-big/) to get started.

No matter how you decide to give back, rest assured you can make a difference — and there are plenty of others out there who will appreciate it. For more ideas, tips, and suggestions, keep reading.

Chapter 2

STAY LOCAL

While people around the world need assistance, you don't have to look far to find people in need. Look in your own community to find plenty of opportunities.

Start Small

It may seem that to truly make a difference you have to dish out tons of money or time. When people think about making a difference, they often think of the bigger groups and organizations that they can work with, volunteer for, or make donations to. But how can you give back if you don't have a lot of money or time to give? You start small.

Sometimes the smallest action or donation can make a huge difference. Just ask the starving man who received a hot meal, the new mother who was able to get an hour of uninterrupted sleep, or the struggling student who got help figuring out a difficult problem. None of these scenarios required a lot of time or money, yet the recipient was more than grateful for the help. Here are some ideas to get you started in your own journey to make a difference:

- Donate to your local food pantry — Go through your kitchen cabinets for non-perishable items that you aren't using (make sure you check expiration dates to ensure they're still good), and donate them to the local food pantry. Or pick up a few staples next time you go grocery shopping and donate those. Some food pantries will also accept donations of toiletry items or even clothing. Contact your local social services department if you aren't sure where the food pantry is or how to donate.

- Donate to charitable organizations — Clothes, housewares, books, and more can be donated to charitable organizations. The items will either be given to those who need them or sold to earn cash that can be used to help others. Clean out your closets and drawers to find items you no longer need or want, and donate these to one such organization. Even larger items, like furniture, can be donated if they're in good condition.

- Donate to a battered women's shelter — Shelters that help victims of domestic abuse can benefit from donations of health and beauty items and clothing items, especially items that can help women establish new lives and careers (i.e. suits for job interviews, etc.). Clean out your closets or pick up a few items on your next shopping excursion.

- Shop at thrift stores — Next time you need to pick up an article of clothing, something for your home, or a new book or movie, swing by your local thrift store. You get what you need, and the money you spend goes toward a worthwhile organization.

- Organize a food or clothing drive — If you're part of a school or organization, put together a drive to gather food or clothing to donate. Have members bring in items to donate, then bring those items over to the food pantry or thrift store. Around the holidays, you can also extend this idea to toy drives for holiday gifts or winter clothing for those in need.

- Organize a blood drive — Contact your local branch of the Red Cross (https://www.redcross.org/find-your-local-chapter.html) to see how you can arrange a blood drive at your school or business.

- Volunteer in small doses — Even an hour or two can help out your local groups and organizations. Volunteer at your local library. See if you can help at a school's homework helpline. Call local organizations that mean something to you: shelters, soup kitchens, animal shelters, etc. They may need help answering phones, filing paperwork, or helping visitors or clients. Any non-profit organization will rely on volunteers to help them function. Call around and find out where you can help.

- Go visiting — Some groups of people would love to simply have someone sit with them for a bit, especially elderly residents at assisted-living complexes and terminally-ill children at hospitals. Taking time to spread some cheer can help them smile and perk up their days a bit. Just be sure to contact the individual locations to find out their guidelines and requirements before stopping by.

- Help your friends and family — Don't forget to look close to home when it comes to helping others. Do you have an elderly neighbor? Offer to shovel snow, cook a meal or two, or help clean house. Know a parent with small children? Offer to babysit so that parent can run errands without a child underfoot or have a date night with their significant other. Or prepare a home-cooked meal or help clean house for new parents. Keep an eye and ear open for opportunities that might help those around you: job openings for your cousin looking for employment, doctor recommendations for a parent whose doctor is retiring, potential customers for your brother starting his own business.

Keep in mind, also, that someone doesn't have to be in need to benefit from a good deed. No matter their lot in life, most people would appreciate a helping hand. Imagine waking up one snowy morning to find your driveway had been shoveled and your car had been brushed off. Imagine opening your door to find a homemade treat resting on your doorstep with a note from your neighbor. Even something as simple as someone taking your garbage cans off the curb can be a pleasant surprise. Anything that eases the burden of those around you and brings a smile to their faces makes a difference. What can you do to help those you care about?

Community Organizations

If you're looking to make a regular, lasting impression on others, look into community organizations. Participating in a community organization can give you the opportunity to use your time and skills to help others through programs and fundraising. And you can be involved over a long period of time, continuing to help even once a specific program or event has ended.

Organizations vary widely, from groups focused on a specific need, such as medical care (i.e. Doctors Without Borders), to those working to solve a specific problem (i.e. American Cancer Society), to those serving a broad range of needs and problems (i.e. Amnesty International). The most important thing is to partner with an organization whose mission and goals match your own. If animals are important to you, for example, working with your local Humane Society may be a good choice.

Below are a few organizations to get you started. Your local community may have additional choices for you. Ask at your local library or do an internet search to find organizations in your area.

- Kiwanis International: https://www.kiwanis.org/

- Rotary International: https://www.rotary.org/en

- American Red Cross: https://www.redcross.org/

- Habitat for Humanity: https://www.habitat.org/

- Heifer International: https://www.heifer.org/

You may also want to look into organizations in your area that serve a specific population, such as people with disabilities, victims of domestic abuse, children, illiterate adults, the homeless, or the unemployed.

Another option is to explore your town's website and check out the many boards and commissions that exist. Many town positions are volunteer-based and can give you a chance to make a different right where you live.

Though it's sad to say, I recommend researching any organizations you haven't heard of before looking to participate. While most organizations you encounter are reputable, many scams exist, as well.

Chapter 3

GOING GLOBAL

If a wider scale effort is more your speed, or you long to see and help the world, you can look beyond your community and find opportunities just about anywhere you can imagine.

As with local opportunities, ways to help tend to fall into two categories: donating and volunteering.

Donating is the simplest, easiest way to contribute if you have the funds. You can reach out to help a country hit by a natural disaster, help third world countries get clean water, food, medical care, and education. Or you can simply donate to an organization you're familiar with and let them decide how to help others.

By choosing to volunteer, you can be the person who actually brings the supplies, food, medical care, and education to people in need. You will be put right in the heart of the communities in need, getting hands-on experience touching the lives of others.

Unless you have personal connections with care efforts, your best bet would be to partner with an organization already working internationally. Some are:

- Peace Corps: https://www.peacecorps.gov/

- AmeriCorps: https://americorps.gov/

- Amnesty International: https://www.amnesty.org/en/

- American Red Cross: https://www.redcross.org/

- Doctors Without Borders: https://www.doctorswithoutbord ers.org/

- Heifer International: https://www.heifer.org/

- Kiwanis International: https://www.kiwanis.org/

- Rotary International: https://www.rotary.org/en

And the list goes on and on. To find organizations that can link you with opportunities, check out:

- VolunteerMatch: https://www.volunteermatch.org/

- Kiva: https://www.kiva.org/

- Global Impact: https://charity.org/

- World Vision: https://www.worldvision.org/

Chapter 4

All About the Kids

Groups and organizations fall into all kinds of categories — and many of them focus on helping children. If you want to make a different in a child's life, you'll find plenty of opportunities, from short-term involvement to a life-long impact.

One important thing to remember when working with children is that these are just kids — meaning they're still vulnerable and impressionable. Your actions can have a greater effect, both positive and negative, than they would with adults, simply because of this. Children will look to you for guidance and knowledge, and how you handle that can determine how these children view you, other adults, and the world.

Working with children requires patience and understanding, especially if you're working with kids who have had to deal with traumatic events, such as illness, abuse, poverty, and homelessness. These events can cause emotional and physical scarring that can affect a child's personality and actions. But, while these scars can make it difficult to get through to a child, your guidance can also have a much greater impact because of them.

If you want to help children but lack the time or understanding to work directly with them, you can consider donating. The organizations that help kids need money to continue, and they often rely on donations to fund some or all of their projects. Find an organization whose mission you can support and give as freely as you can.

For a short-term hands-on commitment, try volunteering with an organization that deals with children, or at public places such as hospitals, schools, and libraries. You can read to kids; help them with their schoolwork; deliver gifts, foods, etc. to sick kids; become a teacher's aide; help organize programs, events, and fundraisers; babysit; and much more.

Mentoring and coaching take volunteering one step further. In addition to helping the children with particular tasks, you're teaching them valuable skills that can have a lasting effect, such as teamwork, self-confidence, leadership, and more, over a period of time. Another option is being a Big with Big Brothers Big Sisters of America (https://www.bbbs.org/) and forming a relationship with a child in need of positive influences.

For a permanent or longer-term impact, you can welcome a child or children into your home through foster parenting or adoption. Not everyone is cut out to be a parent, and even among those who are, many will go through a difficult time that makes them incapable of caring for their children. As such, many kids are in need of loving homes. Not all will have a permanent need; some will be temporary. Those looking for a temporary home would be looking for foster parents, while those needing a permanent family would be looking for adoption.

Foster Parenting

Requirements to qualify to be a foster parent vary from state to state. Contact your local Department of Children and Families to get more information. You'll need to apply to be considered and go through a screening process to verify that you're a responsible adult capable of caring for a child.

Some locations offer a monetary stipend to help care for the children you're responsible for, but don't let that be the deciding factor. Though not permanent, foster parenting is very demanding and not a task to be undertaken lightly. The children going through the system often have emotional scarring and will need patience and understanding as well as love. Be sure you're capable of providing this before taking that step. Also, it can be emotionally trying to have to give the children back at the end of the designated time — especially if you question the parents' ability to care for their children. It's one more thing to consider before deciding to apply.

Foster parenting can be very rewarding, however, and it's a very personal way to make a difference in the lives of others. Children have unique needs, and having a caring role model and caregiver can truly have an impact.

If you think you would like to adopt a child through the foster care program, notify the department so they can pair you with children who are more likely to require adoption rather than temporary care.

Adoption

If you're eager to help children on a more permanent basis, you can also look into adoption. As with foster parenting, it's not a decision to be taken lightly, as children may have special needs or emotional scarring, especially if they're older. And, of course, they need love, support, and care. Taking a child into your family permanently means being there for him or her and providing for that child physically and emotionally.

Adoption can also be expensive, and the wait time for a child can be lengthy, especially if you're looking to adopt a newborn or infant.

For more information and guidance regarding adoption, visit https://adoption.com/.

Chapter 5

MORE INFORMATION

Helping others can be as local or as broad as you'd like it to be. And online resources can help you in your quest, whether it's locating organizations to help or researching a charity before donating. While many individual organizations or charities have their own websites, you can also find general sites that will guide you in your goals.

Finding the Right Charity

If you want to volunteer or donate but don't know where to start, head to a site that reviews many charities in one place. This will help ensure you're working with a reputable charity. Here are some options:

- Charity Navigator: https://www.charitynavigator.org/

- Charity Watch: https://www.charitywatch.org/

- The Life You Can Save: https://www.thelifeyoucansave.org/

- Save.org: https://give.org/

For more ideas on how to make a difference and give back to the world around you, keep your eyes and ears open. Ask around to identify opportunities in your own community. Look for needs that exist in your day-to-day life, whether it's cleaning up trash in the park or offering to help with services you already utilize, such as the public library. For more ideas on how to start small, do an online search for "I want to make a difference" and see what comes up. The possibilities are endless and can be as big or as small as you want them to be.

Part Seven

Staying Motivated

Chapter 1

MOTIVATING YOURSELF

You can be excited to get started, anxious to take those steps toward changing your life. You can really want the end result and picture your life just as you always wanted it. But actually taking those steps, and working toward that end result, can be difficult. Not necessarily because you don't know how to get there, but because you can't get your butt off the sofa to put your plan into action!

Finding a technique to motivate yourself can help get your butt in gear. Sometimes you need a little push, or a reason to get going. While what works for you may differ from what works from me, here are some ideas to get you started.

Books and Movies

Sometimes motivation can come from unlikely sources. Years ago, when my college boyfriend and I broke up, I was pretty upset. I still lived with my parents at the time, and in those days of old-fashioned movie rentals, my mother had rented the movie Legally Blonde. I can't say I was in the mood for a romantic comedy, but I was bored, depressed, and I had wanted to see the movie before we broke up. So I popped it in the DVD player. The result? Best break-up movie ever. At least to me. That movie, more than anything else, gave me the push to get on with my life. It may seem strange, but if you've ever seen the movie, perhaps you understand. If you haven't, I'll give you the quick rundown: girl loves boy, boy breaks up with girl, girl does everything she can to win boy back, boy wants girl back, girl realizes boy isn't worth it. The moral? A relationship does not define who you are as a person.

It makes sense if you think about it. Books and movies are often created from emotion, personal experience, or inspiration. Novels I've written have drawn from my personal experiences and feelings. It's not unreasonable to think that two people will have similar-enough stories that what speaks to one will speak to another. If characters in a book are experiencing life changes, why not use their actions as encouragement for your own? And, as in my own example, if a movie connects with what you're experiencing, why not take it as a kick in the butt for your own goals?

Music and Motivational Audio

When you hear about motivational audio, you probably think of motivational speakers. But, while many people have been helped by experts touting the benefits of thinking positively, believing in yourself, and using your abilities to get ahead, that method doesn't work for everyone. Rest assured, however, that motivational speakers are not the only kind of auditory aid out there.

Personally, I've found great motivation in simply hearing the success stories and tips of others who have traveled the path I'm currently traveling. Knowing that others have succeeded in what I'm trying to do can be tremendously inspiring and can encourage me to push forward more than just about anything else. While you can certainly read about these people, you can also take advantage of driving time and time spent cleaning or doing other mindless tasks by plugging in to podcasts, audio books, and radio programs. With the number of successful people out there, chances are pretty high you'll find a story or situation that resonates with you.

Another option is listening to music. While a lot of music is far from motivational, if you listen to the lyrics of some popular songs, you may find that even famous people have problems — or at least have songwriters who do! Whether they sing about life's issues, being true to yourself, or making changes in their lives, you may be able to connect with and get motivation from these songs if you just pay attention. If that song was inspired by a troubled relationship, and you're going through a similar experience, why not use that song as motivation in your own life?

Here are a few songs I've connected with to get you started. Find them on YouTube, Spotify, or wherever you get your music:

- Keep Your head Up by Andy Grammer

- Firework by Katy Perry

- Hero by Mariah Carey

- Reach by Gloria Estefan

- Man in the Mirror by Michael Jackson

- Live Like You Were Dying by Tim McGraw

- Live Like We're Dying by Kris Allen

- The Climb by Miley Cyrus

Lyrics aside, sometimes just listening to upbeat music can get you in a more positive frame of mind (a big one for me? Shake It Off by Taylor Swift). And positive thinking really can be the best kind of motivation out there.

Pinterest

This unique social media platform gives you the opportunity to create "boards" for just about anything from craft ideas to recipes to funny memes. And if you're looking to make changes in your life, you can use it to really get in touch with what you want and remind yourself of what you're striving for. Think of it as a high-tech vision board.

My first Pinterest board, entitled "Dreams," was used to keep track of things I've achieved and things I'm still hoping to accomplish. I took pictures from my websites and pictures from other websites and other people's boards to view my dreams at a glance. I can see both my successes and goals I'm still working on reaching. If I'm stressed and depressed about something I haven't been able to achieve yet, I can see right next to it a reminder of something great I've accomplished.

If you've ever heard the idea of posting a picture of your goal as motivation to reach it, this works along the same lines. It just takes the concept one step further. Having a visual reminder of what you want can be very powerful motivation indeed. And this gives you the opportunity to add dozens, hundreds, even thousands of reminders. (Just be sure adding pins to your board doesn't become a procrastination tool instead!)

Make a List

I'm a big fan of lists. They're a great way to keep track of what has to get done. But they can also serve another purpose: as a motivational tool. It feels great to check things off! And sometimes that feeling is enough incentive to keep you going.

The important thing to remember when making a list is to be specific. This helps keep you on track by giving you actionable tasks to take care of. Being too vague or too broad will only discourage you — you may not know what to do, or it may take too long to cross anything off. At the same time, don't break things down so far that it gets ridiculous. You want it to mean something when you check an item off.

Start with your overall dream. Then define the goal you're trying to reach in line with that dream. Think about what you need to do to achieve that goal, then break that down into specific, actionable tasks. This may sound familiar, since the process is the same as when you were setting your goals.

Here's an example:

Dream: To be healthy

Goal: To lose 50 pounds

To Do List:

- Work out 5 times by the end of this month

- Work out 10 times next month

- Avoid McDonalds every day for a week

- Avoid McDonalds every day for a month

- Go to the grocery store and buy healthy snacks to bring to work...

You get the idea. You can also play with the format. Rather than have one long list, you can add specific items to your daily planner. Break each step down into manageable chunks and tackle a couple each day. Or you can divide the items on your list into categories and focus on one category at a time, or one item from each category.

Rewards

When you think of rewards, you may think of the trinkets, candy, and stickers you used to get as a kid. While the items may have changed, the concept remains the same: give yourself an incentive for completing a desired action.

Anything that encourages you to complete your goal is fair game. Maybe you just need a sweet treat like a five-year-old would. Or maybe your tastes are a bit more sophisticated, and you need a day of pampering, a trip to the movies, or a new outfit. Whatever it is you decide to offer yourself as a reward, having that incentive can be great motivation.

The important thing to remember, however, is not to sabotage yourself with your rewards. For example: a day of shopping may not be the best reward for paying off that credit card — unless you can pay cash. And indulging in a dessert buffet probably isn't a good idea if your goal is to lose weight.

That being said, take a look at your goals. What is your ultimate dream? What milestones on the way deserve to be rewarded? There are no right or wrong answers here. Whatever gets you moving closer to your goals is perfectly fine. Now think about what you could offer yourself as an incentive that would keep you motivated to push forward, without actually setting you back. Will the rewards get better as you proceed? Will the rewards coordinate with the goal, or will they consist solely of something that makes you happy?

Next, try it out. Offer a reward for your first milestone. Did it offer sufficient incentive, or did you find yourself slacking off? If it's the latter, tweak the reward. Perhaps you didn't want it as much as you thought you did. Keep going until you find a reward system that works for you.

Partner Up

If you can't keep yourself motivated with your own incentives, find someone to be your goal buddy, to keep you motivated and push you along.

Having someone take the journey with you can be a powerful tool. Ideally this person would also be looking to make changes in his or her life, and you could offer encouragement to each other along the way. This partner could help you stay focused and on track, offer incentives to keep you moving forward, and hold you accountable for the goals you set for yourself.

Having a partner can also keep you from feeling alienated and alone. Depending on your goals, you may be lacking in support from other friends and family or simply spending a lot of time on your own. Having someone to turn to and discuss the journey with can prevent you from getting depressed and giving up. And if you feel like you'd be disappointing someone else by not carrying out your goals, you may be more inclined to finish what you started.

So where do you find a partner? Well, you can start by reaching out to friends, family members, colleagues, and others you interact with. If you told them about your life changes, you may be surprised at who else is looking to change their lives, as well. If no one you know is a suitable partner, look online. Forums and Facebook groups can be a great place to meet others in a similar situation as yourself. Search for forums or groups in the particular area you're looking to change. You can also check out sites such as https://www.meetup.com/to connect with others online or in your community. Support groups, if appropriate, can also be valuable resources as you can meet people who are looking for the same things you are. If all else fails, start a blog, and maybe people will come to you!

Chapter 2

The Power Within

Many of us underestimate our abilities. We don't think we're strong enough, smart enough, good-looking enough. We lack the willpower. We lack the proper genes. We weren't born into money. We didn't have opportunities growing up. Does any of this sound familiar?

You're stronger/smarter/better looking/richer than you think you are. When push comes to shove, you could do it if you had to. So why don't you?

It often boils down to one of two things: low self-esteem or a pessimistic attitude. For some, it may be a combination of both. Either way, it will require some re-conditioning to break out of that way of thinking. And you may need help to reaffirm what you tell yourself. But you can do it if you try.

The first step is to recognize when you're slipping into the habit. When are you putting yourself down or underestimating your abilities? What triggers it? Keep track.

Next, take note of how you feel. Often a single negative thought will result in a cascade of pessimism. Suddenly you can't do anything, never mind what you were originally setting out to do. Do you get depressed? Angry? Frustrated? All three?

Now take each negative thought and come up with a counterargument. Instead of thinking about how broke you are, think of how many ways in which you're wealthy (monetarily or not). Instead of bemoaning how you're all alone, think about those who love and respect you. Count your blessings instead of your supposed shortcomings. Trick your mind into thinking positively.

Then, take a deep breath and push the negative thought from your mind. Replace it with an action plan to do what you thought you couldn't. Tell yourself "I can do it!" and prove that you can.

It won't be easy, especially in the beginning. But do this enough, and it will start to become second nature. And you'll begin to tap into the resources you really possess: hidden intelligence, problem-solving abilities, multitasking abilities, time management abilities. You'll discover what you're really capable of achieving. And your goals will be that much closer.

If you find yourself still questioning yourself, or getting hung up on mistakes of the past, doubts, fears, and guilt, you're not alone. And there's nothing wrong with you. It will just take a little more work to get where you want to be.

Doubts

If you make plans, but take no action; dream about a "someday," but take few steps to get there; or simply question whether you're "good enough," "important enough," or "skilled enough," it's likely not your ability that's in question — it's your view of your ability.

It's not easy to overcome this doubt, but I've found that the most effective method is simply forcing yourself to do it. If you want something enough, giving yourself that push to just do it will not only move you closer to your goals; it'll also prove to yourself that you were capable of doing it. It will show that you had the ability — and have the ability — to get where you need and want to be. And the more you do this, the more confidence you'll gain. And that will make it easier to push the doubts aside and really succeed in your goals.

Regrets

I regret taking so long to tackle some of my goals. I regret not taking advantage of time or energy when I had extra. I regret missing out on opportunities because I wasn't willing to take a chance, or because I didn't believe in myself enough.

We all have regrets, whether it's paths we didn't take, paths we *did* take, how we handled something, or just not taking advantage of an opportunity. It's easy to get sucked into the "what if," "might have been," or "could have been." But despite these regrets — or maybe because of them — we have to learn to look forward to what we can actually change, rather than back, to what has already been.

It's easier said than done. But I've found that the easiest, most effective way to accept what has passed is to find the reason for it happening the way it did. It may take some time to find that silver lining, but it's there. Every decision you've made has brought you to this point, and this is where you're meant to be.

- Why did I take so long to start working toward some of my goals? Because I was still learning about myself, about who I am and what I want out of life. I was experiencing things that would get me closer to that.

- Why did I not take advantage of extra time or energy? Because at the time I needed to spend time with my family, or spend some time on self-care, which were more important than getting ahead in other things.

I have found the regrets that tend to linger are the ones I haven't been able to rationalize yet. And, I admit, even some of the ones I have rationalized are still a bit difficult to swallow. But I can't go back and change them.

And neither can you. Just tell yourself that from this point forward, you'll live life to the fullest — and minimize regrets from the past.

Fear

We all have fears. They can be as small as a fear of spiders, or as paralyzing as a fear of leaving the house. These fears can affect our ability to complete the tasks necessary to succeed, and sometimes they can actually set us back. So how do you move past it?

The first step is actually acknowledging the fear. If you don't acknowledge its presence, you won't be able to overcome it. Think about what it is you're afraid of. If you've spent a lot of time suppressing it, this can be more difficult than it seems. But be honest with yourself. Think about the tasks you've been avoiding, the topics or goals you skirt around without meeting head-on. Is the reason for this rooted in fear? Let's use my own experience with my goal of making money (maybe someday a living) from my writing.

- *For me, I think I have a fear of failure — or success, depending on how you look at it. Part of me feels like a fraud, someone who acts like she can do something but actually can't. If I'm truly honest with myself, it's probably the reason my goals take longer than I would like them to. Somehow I think people will catch on to me, that they'll realize I can't really write, that I don't know what I'm doing. And I think that once this happens, I'll fall on my face.*

Once you've acknowledged your fears, try stepping back from them a bit and thinking about them logically. Does it make sense to have that concern? What are the chances that the scenarios you have playing in your head will actually come true? What's the worst that could actually happen?

- *For me, I have to acknowledge that even if I'm not the next best-selling author, there are many who have read my books who tell me I have talent. I'm not a "fraud." And, of course, not everyone will like what I write — even bestsellers have readers who don't care for their works. And plenty of people make a living with their writing in the nonfiction arena who aren't successful in fiction, and I have plenty of ideas there, too.*

Once you've thought about your fears logically, visualize the positive: what good could actually happen from moving past your fears? Can you make it happen? How? When?

- *I could become a successful writer, not tied to a job I may or may not enjoy. I would be able to spend more time with my family, doing something I enjoy, and helping people through my fiction and nonfiction works.*

Last, but not least, tackle your fears! You've done enough thinking. It's time to actually take action and take charge. Even if it's just a baby step, do something that will move you in the right direction.

- *For me, I've started attending more author events, connecting with potential readers and discussing my books. Each one gets a little easier, and I can fit them in around my other responsibilities.*

Even if things don't work out as you would ideally like them to, chances are pretty high that they won't be as bad as you fear they will be. And even when things go wrong, seeing that the end result isn't as traumatic as you thought can actually be therapeutic. You see that your fear was unjustified. And that can help you move even farther and more quickly.

Important Note: If you have a fear that is truly debilitating, such as agoraphobia, you will likely need more help than these tips can provide. I encourage you to reach out to a professional in this field to make strides toward overcoming your fear.

Guilt

Every time I do something that takes me away from my kids, I feel guilty. Every time I choose to do something that doesn't advance one of my goals, I feel guilty. Every time I don't maximize my time, I feel guilty.

Every time I realize that I've made choices that have pulled me farther from my family or professional goals, I feel guilty — even if I made those choices because I didn't have much of a choice at all.

Logically I know there are certain things I have to do in order to take care of my family. I have to spend time cleaning the house so my family is more comfortable. I have to spend time doing things I enjoy because I am not a machine, and I need down time, too.

I'm sure I'm not the only one who feels guilty for some of the things I have to do or choose to do. Sadly, it's a pretty common occurrence in our society. So how do we overcome it?

The most important thing is to stay focused on the big picture. Some of the things that seem incredibly important now won't actually matter in the long run. Many of the day-to-day decisions won't even be remembered in a year or two. As long as I get quality time with my kids, make progress in my goals, and do my best to maintain a work/life balance, the little details aren't that important. The big stuff is taken care of, my kids know I love them, and all of our needs are met. The rest is just extra.

If you're truly doing the best you can, that's all anyone can ask. Do your best to maintain a balance, put in effort on the important things, and avoid getting so wrapped up in your own projects and goals that you exclude everyone and everything else. Stay true to yourself and what's important to you. Keeping the balance between needs and wants will help the big picture remain focused. It will make sure you're not neglecting what has to get done, or your loved ones, or yourself. A little guilt may be inevitable, but try to remember that you're only one person. And that person is doing the best they can.

Chapter 3

DEALING WITH SETBACKS

E ven with a great game plan in place, inspiration to keep you motivated, and rewards here and there as you meet your mini goals, you will experience times when things won't go smoothly. You will encounter setbacks from both external factors and your own internal conflict or reactions.

Setbacks happen. Life happens. But that doesn't mean you should give up. The great thing about taking charge of your life is that even if something happens that sets you back, you can pick yourself up and get yourself back on track. The skills and knowledge you've gained along the way will help you rebuild your confidence and regain your footing.

You are strong enough — and determined enough — to make things happen. Look at yourself and your situation as objectively as possible and acknowledge that things aren't as bad as they seem. Give yourself a pep talk. Your dreams are still within reach. If your goals are important to you, you will find a way to make it work.

External Forces

Sometimes things happen that are out of your control, but they'll have a negative impact on your goals. You don't get that job. Your car breaks down. Your significant other breaks up with you. You get sick, minor or not. An organization you volunteer with doesn't need your help anymore.

These outside factors can set you back a bit and make you feel as if you've taken one step forward only to get pushed two steps back. Rest assured this is normal. Life isn't all smooth sailing. Just think how great it'll feel when things actually go right! These setbacks will help you appreciate the positive when it happens. But in the meantime, do the best you can to muddle through. If you need to wallow a bit, take that time to wallow. Just make sure you're ready to pick yourself up and push forward again when the wallowing is done.

The external forces that have the biggest impact tend to fall into one of three categories: health, relationships, and money. Whether or not your goal involves any of these, they will likely impact whatever projects, goals, and dreams you have. While we may not be able to control those crises that pop up, we can set ourselves up for success by minimizing the impact they have overall.

Health

Being sick greatly affects your ability to accomplish anything on your to do list, never mind your overall goals. If you're feeling under the weather, you will likely have to stick to the bare minimum to make it through each day. At times when you feel a bit better, you can attempt to make progress on your tasks, but the best bet is usually to let your body rest and recuperate. Doing so will help ensure you get back on your feet as soon as possible. Trying to push yourself too much usually results in further setbacks that actually delay the process even more. So, rule of thumb? Let your body recover without pressure.

If a long-term illness or disease sets you back, you may need to partner with your healthcare providers to determine your limits. You may find yourself having good days and bad days, moments of weakness and moments of renewed energy. Work with what your body is telling you and give yourself some grace. As with a temporary illness, pushing yourself too hard will likely only make things worse. Only you know what you can handle, but make sure you're listening to your body and not just your desire to be productive.

Once you're feeling better, then you can get back on track with your tasks and goals. If your illness is long-term, then look for times when you feel physically up to tackling tasks.

To minimize the effects of illness, a general best practice is to keep yourself as healthy as possible. Maintaining a healthy diet, exercising regularly, and following healthcare providers' recommendations will help keep you in your best possible health, and help reduce the number of times you get sick. Try not to push yourself too hard, as fatigue and stress can make you more susceptible to getting sick, too. Try to give yourself breaks and maintain balance in your life.

Relationships

While we want to have healthy, strong relationships with others, on occasion certain relationships will be toxic, sabotaging our chances of success and overall making us disgruntled and miserable.

As we discussed in the Relationships section, only you can decide what kind of relationships you want to have with others. If someone has caused you pain or discomfort, has offended you, or has done something you don't agree with, only you can decide how it will affect your relationship with that person. Can you forgive and forget? Will it have lasting consequences? Was the situation too much for you to tolerate? These setbacks must be handled on a case-by-case basis, and I encourage you to review the ideas and suggestions in the Relationships section for more guidelines.

In a more general sense, interactions with other people can affect our day-to-day lives and how well we're able to move forward. Everyone has a life. And those lives come complete with problems, relationships, changes, jobs, and more. In a word, they come with drama. And it's easy to get sucked into the drama that is everyone else's life — and lose track of your own life in the meantime.

So how do you move past the drama and focus on your own issues? You start by minding your own business.

This doesn't mean don't have an interest in other people or what's going on in their lives. Especially if you're friends with them or interact with them on a regular basis, you'll want to chat often and stay updated on the latest happenings. But hearing bits of news (and responding appropriately to them) and letting that news *affect* you are two different things. Lend an ear, offer support, but keep your distance when it comes to getting intimately involved — especially if that involvement involves criticizing, gossiping, or badmouthing. Do you really need to add fuel to the fire by criticizing your coworker's boyfriend? Do you need to jump on the bandwagon and make fun of your son's teacher's haircut?

If you find yourself criticizing and judging everyone else, whether or not others are, too, take a look at your own life. Chances are there's something lacking that's causing you to lash out at others. You try to make yourself feel better by "proving" that others' lives aren't perfect, either. But all this does is make you bitter and cynical — and often even more miserable. Instead, try to look at the positive in others. Doing so may make you less critical of yourself, as well, and can give you a more positive outlook on your own life. If you find this too difficult, try to ignore the people or situations causing your judgement.

Once you've made the decision to not create or get sucked into the drama, try steering conversation in a more positive direction. If you've having difficulty with this, try avoiding the negative conversation. If someone is talking negatively or chatting about others behind their backs, make an excuse and walk away. Don't ask questions that will invite critical comments. Avoid discussing trigger topics or people. Over time the people who bring the drama will learn that you're not interested. And that will make everyone's lives more pleasant!

Money

Big, unexpected expenses can greatly derail our plans and progress. Whether you no longer have the funds to finance your plans or you need to find ways to earn money quick, thus reducing the time you have available to work on your plans, money can cause big problems when it comes to your goals. And if your goals are directly related to money, those problems can be magnified.

Having an emergency fund can help alleviate these problems as they come up, so try to get ahead of unexpected expenses by tucking money aside when you can. If you don't yet have an emergency fund, however, or if the expenses are higher than what you have available, you'll need to determine a course of action. Consider this setback a new goal and proceed accordingly. Start the process from the beginning, determining what needs to change, how you want it to change, and what steps you'll need to take to make that change happen. Then take the steps one at a time.

Huge setbacks aside, money seems to have taken over our society so it's impossible to get much done without it. And a lack of money can impact how and when we're able to progress. But that doesn't mean it has to completely control our lives. You can find free resources to help you in your goals, or you can find ways to save on your expenses so you can fund your dreams.

Free Resources

When it comes to free resources, you can find many places to visit online that can help you with your goals, whether they're informational sites, blogs, or forums. But you can find many local resources, as well:

- Your local library — Not only does the library offer books and magazines on just about every topic imaginable; it can also help you in the form of reference librarians who can help guide you in the right direction. Libraries also offer free tools such as computers with internet access for those who may not have them at home, or DVDs for both entertainment and informational purposes. And check out library programs such as workshops and lectures that can offer additional information and guidance for your journey.

- Clubs and organizations — Whether it's a career path you want to pursue or a volunteer opportunity you'd like to participate in, local clubs and organizations can offer you options, feedback, and networking possibilities.

- Support groups — Health changes, relationship concerns, money issues — you'll find support groups for all of them. Whether it's kicking a drug addiction, struggling with the illness or loss of a loved one, or fighting the urge to shop or gamble, a support group can offer much needed assistance to reach your goal. Conduct an internet search to find local groups or reach out to your local social services department.

- Nature — While you may think of it if you're looking to lose weight by exercising, a walk through nature can also help you in other ways. Being surrounded by calming views, scents, and sounds can ease stress and clear your mind so you're able to focus on the problems at hand. Freeing your mind can help you think of creative ways to deal with your concerns, or even present new questions or ways of looking at things to help you in your quest.

Saving Money

Chances are you can save money in just about any aspect of your life that requires you to spend money, whether it's food, clothing, recreation, or household bills. By saving a little here and there, you can free up extra money to find your goals. Below are some ideas on how to cut back.

- Save on groceries — Shop sales and partner those sale prices with coupons. Stock up on items you use frequently to avoid last-minute trips to the store. Shop around to find the stores that have the lowest prices on what you use the most.

- Save on clothing — Consider secondhand stores, discount chains, and outlets. Shop sales to save money — but don't be swayed by supposed savings. Only purchase items you need and will wear. Avoid trends to keep your clothes wearable longer.

- Save on entertainment — Check out your local area to find free entertainment, such as concerts or museums. Explore nature or participate in sports with friends and community organizations. Look for ways to save, such as happy hour specials or AAA discounts. Try hitting the library for the latest DVDs instead of streaming.

- Save on household bills — Shop around for the lowest rates on heating oil, electricity, cable, etc. Ask your current supplier to match rates offered by another. Adjust your thermostat so the heat or central air doesn't kick on as often. Ask your credit card companies for a lower rate. Take a good look at your bills to see if there are features you're paying for but aren't using — and get rid of them!

Internal Reactions

Let's face it, we're not perfect. We will on occasion slip a little in our goals and do something that will contradict what we're trying to achieve, whether it's splurging on that chocolate cake, buying a gadget we really didn't need, or wasting time zoning out to the TV. The actual act, while not productive, is not the real concern. The concern is what we do after it happens.

It's going to happen. Don't beat yourself up about it. Repeat: don't beat yourself up about it. The harder you are on yourself, the worse you'll feel, and the harder it will be to get yourself back on track. Now that's not saying you can just throw caution to the wind and do whatever you feel like. If you're serious about turning things around and taking charge of your life, you'll need to do the right thing most of the time. But cutting yourself some slack when you slip up will make it easier to stay on track the rest of the time. If you allow yourself a little freedom, you won't feel as restricted — and you won't feel the need to rebel with more constant slip-ups.

If you find yourself slipping up often, ask yourself why. Maybe you're trying to tackle too much at a time. Maybe you're trying to take steps that are just too drastic. Cut back a little, make your efforts a bit smaller, and see if you can do better. Baby steps will still get you there. It may take a little longer, but if you're frequently setting yourself back, those big steps aren't getting you there any faster anyway! It's all about finding the right pace for you, so you can keep yourself in the right frame of mind.

- Maybe cutting out all extra spending at once is too much. Try just cutting out one daily or weekly expense to start with.

- Maybe cutting out all sweets is too dramatic. Try limiting yourself to one or two a day instead.

- Maybe expecting to ace all your classes is too much pressure. Try your best, study for your test, and see how well you do. Or maybe take less classes at a time so you can better focus on each one.

If the cause of the slip-ups is that progress seems slow, or outside factors seem to be against you so you can barely tread water, never mind move ahead, you may find yourself reacting with negative thoughts. And this can lead to bouts of depression, whether you're normally prone to them or not. Fortunately, you have several options to try to get yourself out of your funk. Check out Part Four Chapter 4 for suggestions.

Note: I want to remind you that I am not a doctor. If you have depression that is based on a chemical imbalance, not on a depressing situation, I encourage you to seek medical attention.

If you feel in control, but you're just not making any progress, evaluate your situation. What's holding you back? Is it time? Money? Motivation? Or does it just seem that no matter how hard you try you're just not getting anywhere? Think through your concerns, and read through this book for additional guidance. Take a deep breath, reevaluate your game plan, and take baby steps in the right direction. It will take time and patience, but this, too, shall pass.

Sometimes, if things seem to be at a bit of a standstill, and I'm not getting anywhere, I like to think of it as the calm before the storm. Yes, things are quiet and unproductive now, but any day now the tides will change, and I'll make incredible progress in my goals. Inspiration, time, and results will all come together to create a much-needed downpour after a drought.

How is this helpful? Well, it can be a self-fulfilling prophecy. If I'm convinced things will get more interesting, then I'm more motivated to get things done. Getting things done helps ensure I move forward in my goals, which can then result in a flurry of progress and a spike in production — the "storm."

Internal Conflict

External setbacks and even your reactions to them are relatively easy to handle — when compared to turmoil of your own making. Struggling with your choices — determining whether you made the right decision, figuring out what's really important to you, all while balancing the demands of life — is perhaps the greatest challenge of all.

In novel writing, it's very important to make sure your characters have depth, that they're not two-dimensional stereotypes. How is this relevant? Well, the reason we want characters with depth is that they more closely resemble real people. They're relatable. In life, people are rarely driven by a singular focus. We have different aspects of our lives and values: our family self, our worker self, our individual self, our friend self. When we determine our courses of action, we take into consideration not only how they affect us personally, but how they affect those around us, as well. The people we socialize with, work with, and live with impact what we do and how we live.

As such, we may find ourselves at times divided. What will please one group of people or one aspect of our lives may not please another. Or what pleases the people we associate with may not be the best option for us personally. Similarly, if you want to change more than one aspect of your life, chances are you will encounter times when those wants conflict. In other words, moving forward in one of your goals will create a problem with another one of your goals. How do you handle that? How do we determine what to do? What is the best choice?

A Decision to Make

For me, one such time came when I was about four months pregnant with my first child. Obviously having this child was very important to me. My husband and I were very anxious to be parents, and we had been trying for a while. At the same time, I was trying to establish myself as a writer, working on writing and marketing my novels, creating a website, and writing articles for another site. One would think that the two would have little to no effect on each other. My body was taking care of the baby making, and any free time I had was being filled with writing endeavors. No problem.

Well, no problem — until the baby making took its toll on my body. I was exhausted, unmotivated, and lazy. I wanted nothing more than to sit and watch movies all day. Not exactly a great idea when I have a career to get off the ground! My plans were thrown into upheaval, and I found myself getting more and more behind in my goals. What could I do?

I had to make a choice.

When your wants conflict, you simply have to decide what's more important (simple to say, not necessarily easy to do!). Which want is more pressing, more vital to your happiness? For me, I could push myself harder, get my work done, but continue to add strain to my body. I would likely move forward in my career goals, but there was the chance it would have a negative impact on my baby. Or, I could take it easy, let my body do what it had to do, and cut myself some slack on the other goals. I chose to put my baby first. Yes, I got behind on my career goals. But I didn't want to do anything to harm my baby. That was more important to me than advancing my career.

Only you can make the decision as to what's right for you. Perhaps your choice would have been different than mine. Perhaps you will find yourself more conflicted, unsure which path to choose. It may not be easy. But ultimately you have to do what will make you the happiest. If something had happened to my baby because I had pushed myself too hard, I never would have been able to live with myself. Will you be able to live with your decision?

The answer can come only after reflection and processing, weighing the options, and carefully considering the best choice. Maybe the solution involves the items in conflict taking turns, with each one taking priority at different times. Or maybe you'll discover that one of them wasn't that important to you after all. Do your best to determine the best solution for you.

Setting Priorities

Chances are your choices will not be a matter of life and death. Few choices are. But knowing your priorities, and which goals mean more to you, can help make your decision easier. It can also help you figure out what to focus on so you don't get overwhelmed trying to change everything at once. Which want do you want to change the most?

It may help you as you go if you sit down and list everything you're looking to change — no matter how big or small. Then, place them in order of importance. What are you looking to change first? What can wait a while? What will have the biggest impact on your life? Does one thing have to be done before another? Prioritize a bit, and those conflicts may be easier to resolve.

Missing Your Goals

Even when you know what you have to do, it's possible you won't reach your goals. Things happen. Life gets in the way, or the motivation to push through is simply not there. So what do you do to keep moving forward?

Ask yourself why

Why didn't you reach your goal? Did something happen that prevented you from taking the necessary steps? Was it an unreasonable goal? Or did you just lack the motivation to keep going?

Determine a course of action

Once you've determined why you didn't reach your goal, come up with a list of steps so you can still reach that goal — even if the deadline needs to be changed or the goal needs to be adjusted:

- If something happened to hinder you, make adjustments so you can be successful. Did you need more time? More information? Was something else going on in your life that took away your focus? Even if it means stepping away for a bit, assess what it is you need to reach your goal.

- If the goal was unreasonable or unrealistic, make adjustments so it's more practical. Perhaps you need more time to complete the steps. Perhaps you need to break the goal into smaller, more manageable chunks. Or perhaps the goal itself needs tweaking to make it achievable.

- If you lacked the motivation to keep going, ask yourself why. Did you not really care about your goal? Is it something you actually wanted? Were other things happening in your life that distracted you? Did pushing forward require more willpower and effort than you had at the time? If you're no longer interested in your goal, that's okay. Remember: this is your life, and you can make the goals you want. You're not obligated to stick with your first game plan. If, however, life just got in the way, come up with a new plan to allow you to still reach that goal on a more extended time table.

Learn from the experience

Once you've resolved the issue with this goal, look at your other goals. What can you do to make yourself more successful with those goals? How can you set yourself up for success next time? Even if it's too late to make this goal happen as planned, learning from the experience can help ensure your next goals are reached as smoothly as possible.

Back-Up Plans

We'd all love to reach our goals as quickly as possible. We want to be happy, and to be living the lives we want to be living. Unfortunately, this isn't always possible, at least not as quickly as we would like. Sometimes sacrifices need to be made, especially when we have priorities and not everything can be done at once.

For me, I would love to be a work-at-home mom, working as a writer. But life happens, and finances won't let me make that step. So I've had to make sacrifices. To keep a roof over our heads and make sure my kids have the opportunity to grow and flourish, I have to maintain a full-time job. Do I attempt to get a work-from home job, knowing I will likely really hate the options available to me? Or do I pursue a career that takes me out of the home but brings me fulfillment? I opted for the latter, knowing that a happy mom is important, and working yet another job that made me miserable would have negative impacts not only on my kids but on life in general.

Were there other options? Maybe. At the time, I made the best choice I could, and it has worked out pretty well. If a better solution presents itself later, I know I can always make changes, once I've evaluated the options and made the right choice for my family at that time.

To determine the right choice for you, it can be helpful to have a back-up plan when creating your goals, especially if you're dealing with deadlines. If for whatever reason you don't reach your goal, what will you do?

In my example, I knew I had other options, other jobs I could look into or other career options to pursue if the one I chose didn't work out. When I decided to start a new career, as a librarian, I also knew that even if I decided the focus I chose (youth services) wasn't a good fit, my new degree would serve me well in other areas of librarianship, as well. In other words, I had back-up plans upon back-up plans.

Think about your goals, about what you want to achieve. Do you have a deadline? Is there a certain point when you'll have to make an adjustment, no matter what? Will the money run out? Time run out? Patience run out? Think about what you'll do if you do need to make an adjustment. Is there tweaking that can be done to keep you moving in the right direction? Can you push that deadline back a bit? Can you do something temporary to enable you to make a big push again in a few days, weeks, months?

Knowing what you'll do in the event that things don't work out according to plan can save you a lot of stress. It doesn't mean you have to give up on your dreams or your goals. It just means that as the deadline looms, you don't have to put as much pressure on yourself (unless you want to). You'll know that no matter what happens, you know what to do. Don't consider it a failure if you need to use this back-up plan. It's there for a reason. And who knows — if everything happens for a reason, maybe it'll be a blessing in disguise

Stepping Back

As committed as you are to your goals, as dedicated as you may be to the process, there will likely come a time when you want to throw in the towel. If your ultimate goal is worthwhile, it has probably been a struggle to proceed. You get frustrated and discouraged. Even the small victories don't seem frequent enough to keep you going.

When these times rear their ugly heads, step back for a moment. Cut yourself some slack. Anything worth achieving will take effort, and that effort may seem monumental at times. Rather than let the frustration get the best of you, take a breather. Whether it's for a few minutes, a few days, or a week or more, taking a break from the work can help you regain perspective. It's not failing to need time away. You're not giving up. You're just taking a much-needed vacation. It can be difficult to remember why you're working so hard when you're in the heat of the moment.

When you're taking that break, evaluate what has taken place so far. Are you pleased with your progress? Are your goals still the same? Do you still want the same things?

If you find you still want the same things, great! Use the time away from your struggles to reevaluate your plans, make necessary adjustments, and regain the passion you once had. The time away can motivate you more than pushing through would.

If, however, your point of view has changed, that's okay, too. It's okay if you don't want the same things anymore. The path that led you to want to change your life has led you here, too. Maybe your plans need tweaking. Maybe your goals need adjusting. It's okay. No one said you had to achieve *that* goal. It's your dream, after all. If your dream has changed, change it! Think about what you want. Create a new goal. Make a new plan.

You may feel like the time and effort you've put in thus far have been a waste if you change your mind. Was all that energy spent for nothing? Try looking at it this way: if you hadn't put in that effort, you wouldn't have come to this conclusion. Perhaps you would still be wondering "what if?" and struggling with not achieving your goal. By having tried and determining your desires lie elsewhere, you haven't failed. You've simply come to an alternate conclusion. It's like a science experiment that doesn't have the expected results. It's not a failed experiment — it's an experiment with unexpected results. And those results can be just as important. What have you learned about yourself in the meantime? Is there something else you'd like to try instead? Do you have a new goal in mind?

The most important thing is to stick with it. Even if things don't go according to plan, you're moving in the right direction, taking charge of your life, and creating the life you want. And you can learn a lot as you're going. If you look at each step of the process as a learning experience and positive action, you may find it a bit easier to accept life when things don't go very well. Look back at what you've accomplished thus far and think about what you can take from it. What have you learned about yourself, about your goals, and about the people in your life? What would you change? What are you happy with?

After you've evaluated the past, look to the future — and grab hold of whatever new dreams you're reaching for.

Chapter 4

DEALING WITH SUCCESS

With hard work and perseverance, you will be successful. And success should be celebrated. But success can look and feel different than we thought it would. How will *you* deal with your success?

Victories Along the Way

Even if your end goal is far away, and the path to get there riddled with potholes and thunderstorms, you will encounter small victories along the way that can keep you motivated and pushing through.

The small victories you encounter may be planned or unplanned. You may have set smaller goals as milestones to celebrate as you go. Or fate may be kind and offer you an opportunity ready to grab. Perhaps a position opened up that would be perfect for you. Perhaps a friend or family member just shared a bit of good news. Perhaps the perfect mate just happened to cross your path. Whatever the happy accident, celebrate it! Take a moment to savor the occasion. Enjoy the feeling of accomplishment. Then reward yourself for the excellent progress you're making.

Reaching Your Goals

If you're anything like me, you've got a bunch of different goals going at once. Life is not so simple that it has a single focus. With that being said, it makes sense that you'll reach your goals at different points in time. Perhaps one of your victories along the way is actually one of your dreams coming true. What happens then?

By all means, enjoy the achievement! but recognize that it may impact not only your life as a whole, but also the progress you've been making on your other goals. Success in one area may mean a setback in another.

- One of my big goals was to start a family. Having my first child was a huge goal accomplished. But he took up a lot of time and energy, and my other goals took a beating. At the same time, both my kids have become great motivation to work harder and get to where I want to be.

- Perhaps you've finally landed your dream job, but the extra hours may put a strain on your relationships, health, etc. How will you adjust your life to accommodate the new position?

- Maybe you've found your life's mate, but relationships take time. How will you stay on track to find that new career, keep up with your volunteer work, and maintain your exercise regimen?

The changes are not necessarily negative, but they will require adjustments, modifications, and perhaps reworking of your game plans and goals. Even when dreams start coming true, the work isn't over!

Be Realistic

Have you ever given thought to what life will be like when you accomplish all your goals? I bet if you have, you're picturing a rosy, perfect life filled with happiness and joy, right? Now get realistic and think about what it'll *really* be like. Where will the results of your actions lead you?

Starting a family was a dream come true — but it came with sleepless nights, mess and noise, stress and worry. Changing my career brought me fulfillment in some respects, a good, steady paycheck, the opportunity to help others and make a difference, but it also brought coworker drama, some downsides I hadn't anticipated in the job itself, and took me away from my family more hours than I would like.

Where will your goals lead you?

I'm not trying to discourage you from accomplishing your goals. I just don't want you to think that the goal is the only thing to think about. If you focus only on one thing, one point in time, you'll be disappointed — not only on the way there as you're frustrated with not being there yet, but also when you get there and realize it's not everything you had imagined in your rosy picture. Being realistic will keep you grounded, and keep you focused on what's really important. Life is filled with good and bad, in balance. As long as there's more good than bad, I'd say you're pretty lucky!

In the meantime, while you're striving for your goals, you can also prepare yourself to make your imagined reality even more pleasant. Being realistic will help you lay the foundation for a happier life, as you set yourself up for success instead of disappointment. There will be a lot of good moments, worthwhile moments, that make you happy. But accepting that it won't all be perfect will help make the wonderful little moments all that much sweeter.

Chapter 5

Live in the Moment

While taking charge of your life is certainly hard work, that doesn't mean you can't enjoy yourself on the way. Staying focused on the end result is great, and can keep you motivated to push forward, but don't forget to live your life as you're working. Life is precious, and we never know what tomorrow will bring. Be sure to enjoy the bits of happiness that come your way.

As hard as it may seem during moments of frustration, you will have times of contentment. They may be fleeting and rare, but you will come across moments when everything seems to be going well.

Enjoy these moments as they come. You've earned them. You've been working hard, and these moments of contentment are proof that you're headed in the right direction. If you can have, even just for a moment, a bit of happiness, your dreams will seem that much closer. And just a single moment can boost your spirits like nothing else.

It's easy to get stressed out by putting too much pressure on yourself. Doing so will ensure you'll never be content. Allow yourself to step back and live. Take a deep breath, look around at all you have to be thankful for, and think about what you're really doing all this for.

As you move closer to your goals, and find yourself meeting more mile-stones and accomplishing more of your mini goals, moments of con-tentment will become more frequent. That's when you'll feel like you're really getting somewhere: when the dream is within reach and everything just clicks. Until that day, savor the feeling and look forward to the day when all your hard work will have been worth it.

Notes

Novels by

Vanessa E. Kelman

Fate Trilogy

Chasing Fate
Accepting Fate
Tempting Fate

Pine Valley

Searching for Home
Between the Moments

For more information, visit www.VanessaKelman.com.